I, Me, You, We

Advanced Curriculum From Vanderbilt University's Programs for Talented Youth

I, Me, You, We

Individuality Versus Conformity

ELA Lessons for Gifted and Advanced Learners in Grades 6–8

Emily Mofield, Ed.D.,
& Tamra Stambaugh, Ph.D.

Routledge
Taylor & Francis Group

NEW YORK AND LONDON

First published in 2016 by Prufrock Press Inc.

Published 2021 by Routledge
605 Third Avenue, New York, NY 10017
2 Park Square, Milton Park, Abingdon, Oxon OX14 4RN

Routledge is an imprint of the Taylor & Francis Group, an informa business

ISBN 13: 978-1-0321-4388-0 (hbk)
ISBN 13: 978-1-6182-1495-9 (pbk)

DOI: 10.4324/9781003235620

Table of Contents

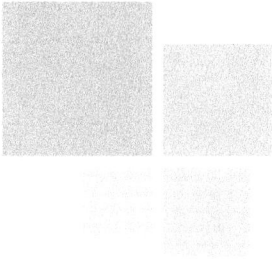

Dedication

To my former students. Your joyful love of learning continues to inspire me.
—Emily

To my nieces and nephews and other gifted students I have worked with who need an accelerated curriculum to stay engaged and to grow in their learning.
—Tamra

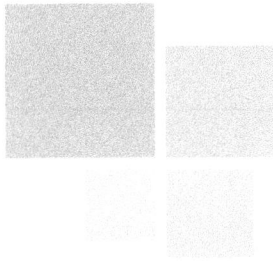

Acknowledgements

We would like express heartfelt gratitude to those dedicated administrators and teachers who implemented the lessons and provided valuable feedback for revisions. You know who you are and we are most grateful! We especially want to recognize Emilie Hall for organizing data and fine-tuning lessons during the editing process. Dr. Elizabeth Covington is appreciated for her professional insight into the development of the literary and rhetorical analysis models to verify the scholarly validity of their use. We also appreciate the work of our editor, Katy McDowall, for her steadfast work and patience as we continued to fine-tune lessons and ask questions well into the editing process. Finally, we are honored to build these lessons on a solid foundation of knowledge, theory, and best practices in gifted education and curriculum development established from the inspiring work of Dr. Joyce VanTassel-Baska.

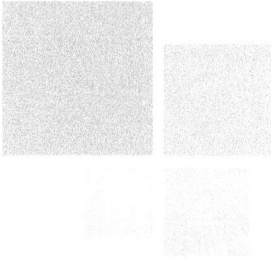

Introduction

I, Me, You, We: Individuality Versus Conformity is designed specifically with gifted and high-achieving middle and early high school learners in mind. These concept-based lessons are accelerated beyond typical grade-level standards and include advanced models to help students analyze a variety of texts. Students explore essential questions such as: How does our environment shape our identity? What are the consequences of conforming to a group? When does social conformity go too far? This unit includes a major emphasis on rigorous evidence-based discourse through the study of common themes across rich, challenging nonfiction and fiction texts. Aligned to the Common Core State Standards (CCSS), the unit guides students to examine the fine line between individuality and conformity through the related concepts of belongingness, community, civil disobedience, self-reliance, and questioning the status quo by engaging in creative activities, Socratic seminars, literary analyses, and debates. Lessons include close readings with text-dependent questions, choice-based differentiated products, rubrics, formative assessments, and ELA tasks that require students to analyze texts for rhetorical features, literary elements, and themes through argument, explanatory, and prose-constructed writing. The unit features short stories from Kurt Vonnegut and Ray Bradbury, poetry from Emily Dickinson and Maya Angelou, art by M. C. Escher and Pablo Picasso, and primary source documents from Plato, Eleanor Roosevelt, William Bradford, Ralph Waldo Emerson, and Henry David Thoreau.

CONCEPTUAL FRAMEWORK

I, Me, You, We: Individuality Versus Conformity is one of four units designed specifically for gifted middle school students (grades 6–8) to support the acquisition of textual analysis skills including identifying the relationship between literary elements within a text, evaluating arguments, enhancing thinking and communication skills, and connecting conceptual generalizations from cross-curricular themes through a variety of media including literary texts, art, and primary source

1 DOI: 10.4324/9781003235620-1

2

documents. The Integrated Curriculum Model (ICM; VanTassel-Baska, 1986) is the conceptual framework used for the unit design. Components of the framework are embedded in each lesson: accelerated content, advanced literacy processes of the discipline (e.g., rhetorical analysis and literary analysis), and conceptual understandings. For example, the accelerated content includes ELA (English language arts) standards, aligned to the CCSS. The CCSS selected for each unit are above the grade level(s) for which the unit was intended. Each unit also includes process skills and specific models to help students evaluate the development of effective arguments; analyze a variety of texts, art, and primary sources; and connect literature to real-world applications (see Appendices A and B for more information on the models). The content of each lesson is connected by an overarching theme and key generalizations that span a variety of disciplines. These concepts vary by unit and include power, truth versus perception, individuality versus conformity, and freedom. Table 1 shows how each unit in this series aligns with the ICM features. The ICM model was selected based on its evidence-supported success in increasing gifted student achievement (see VanTassel-Baska & Stambaugh, 2008).

INTENDED GRADE LEVEL(S)

It is well known in gifted education that accelerated content is essential for increasing the academic achievement and social-emotional growth of gifted students (Assouline, Colangelo, VanTassel-Baska, & Lupkowski-Shoplik, 2015; Colangelo, Assouline, & Gross, 2004; Steenbergen-Hu & Moon, 2011). This unit is intended for and has been piloted with gifted students in grades 6–8. The unit is aligned to CCSS standards primarily focused on grades 9–10 with some lower grade standards included as needed. The accelerated content is necessary so that gifted students have the opportunity to gain new language arts content knowledge at a pace and level that is appropriate for their learning needs. Gifted students' readiness and experience levels vary, as do their abilities. Because school contexts and content emphases are different, it is up to each teacher to determine which unit is best suited for their particular students and at which grade levels. Some gifted students may find this unit engaging as a sixth grader while others may need to wait until grade 7 or 8 to fully participate and understand the unit concepts. Teachers of 9th and 10th graders may find that these units are on target for many of their general education students.

Table 1
The Integrated Curriculum Model Alignment by Unit

Unit	Accelerated Content	Advanced Processes Models/Organizers	Concept/Generalizations
Finding Freedom	Aligned to grade 9 and 10 CCSS standards	Advanced Models: ▪ Social Studies Connections ▪ Rhetorical Analysis Organizers: ▪ Reasoning About a Situation or Event ▪ Big Idea Reflection: Primary Sources	▪ Freedom requires sacrifice. ▪ Freedom requires responsibility. ▪ Freedom is threatened by internal and external forces.
Perspectives of Power	Aligned to grade 9 and 10 CCSS standards	Advanced Models: ▪ Literary Analysis ▪ Visual Analysis ▪ Rhetorical Analysis Organizers: ▪ Big Idea Reflection ▪ Reasoning About a Situation or Event	▪ Power is the ability to influence. ▪ Power is connected to a source. ▪ Power may be used or abused.
I, Me, You, We: Individuality Versus Conformity	Aligned to grade 9 and 10 CCSS standards	Advanced Models: ▪ Literary Analysis ▪ Visual Analysis ▪ Rhetorical Analysis Organizers: ▪ Big Idea Reflection ▪ Reasoning About a Situation or Event	▪ Both conformity and individuality are agents of change. ▪ Both conformity and individuality involve sacrifice. ▪ There are positives and negatives to both conformity and individuality.
In the Mind's Eye: Truth Versus Perception	Aligned to grade 9 and 10 CCSS standards	Advanced Models: ▪ Literary Analysis ▪ Visual Analysis ▪ Rhetorical Analysis Organizers: ▪ Big Idea Reflection ▪ Reasoning About a Situation or Event	▪ Although truth is constant, one's perception of truth varies. ▪ There are negatives and positives in realizing the truth. ▪ There are consequences to believing perception rather than the truth.

LESSON FORMAT AND GUIDELINES

Each lesson in this unit follows a similar format for ease of use. Teachers select from a variety of questions, activities, and differentiated products to best meet their students' needs.

Alignment to Standards

The unit incorporates the key pedagogical shifts highlighted as part of the CCSS. For example, students read both literary and informational texts from a variety of sources and perspectives. Through the use of primary sources, they learn domain-specific content from their readings and are required to provide text-based evidence to support their answers or ideas. Each lesson also supports opportunities for students to make or analyze an argument, defend a position, or interpret a text. Of course, part of close reading and understanding of a text includes the use of domain-specific vocabulary. The readings selected throughout the unit build upon specific concepts and highlight multiple perspectives. Many readings use vocabulary of the time period or a specific discipline, for which students must understand and define.

The beginning of each lesson includes a list of the overarching goals and objectives as well as CCSS specific to each lesson. The end of the unit includes a CCSS alignment chart (p. 205). This unit was not designed to meet every CCSS ELA standard for a particular grade level.

Materials

When differentiating for the gifted, it is important for the materials and readings to be at a level commensurate with the student's ability. The readings and resources in this unit have been carefully selected and include either sophisticated concepts or reading selections above most middle school grade levels. The materials section includes a list of resources needed for the lesson. Some of the listed materials are optional and many of the selected texts, visuals, or videos are readily available online as a free download. When possible, reliable sites and specific links, available at the time of this unit's printing, are provided. *A word of caution*: It is important to note that some of the readings may be controversial or contain advanced or sensitive concepts and content. A cautionary note is provided in lessons with the most controversial issues. Still, it is up to the teacher and school administration to understand the context of his or her district and to determine whether or not a reading or discussion is appropriate or whether a different text or discussion-based question should be used. As the lessons follow a specific format and the analysis models can be used with any text, teachers may easily substitute a more appropriate source and then apply questions and activities for that source using a selected analysis model as a guide (see Appendix A for specific descriptions of each model).

Introductory Activities

The introductory activities provide a real-world connection or "hook" that sets the tone for the remainder of the lesson and enhances student engagement. Sample options include quick debates about an issue or dilemma, symbol designs to illustrate a key concept or idea, or key discussion questions that help students better understand the relevance of a lesson's text, art, or primary source.

Text-Dependent Questions for Close Reading

This section provides questions that ensure students understand the text. These close reading questions are varied and the majority focus on comprehension and inference making. Students are to answer these questions using textual evidence. Note that prediction or speculation questions that cannot be supported with evidence from the text are not appropriate for this section. A variety of questions are listed, but not all questions should be asked in a given lesson. Instead, teachers select four to six questions from the list for students to discuss in small groups, Socratic seminars, or as an entire class. Of course, if students are struggling to understand the text, additional questions or background information may be required. The questions in this section are *not* intended as homework or to be responded to in writing on a consistent basis. These questions are designed for discussion purposes so that teachers can check for understanding and help students support new ideas or clarify misunderstandings.

Analysis Section

This is the most comprehensive and complex section of each lesson and includes a variety of advanced processes and specific models so that students make real-world connections to big ideas and better analyze literature, rhetorical arguments, and visual prompts. These models were created after extensive research and consultation with an English language arts expert to ensure content validity. See Appendix A for a detailed explanation, instructions, and an example lesson using each model.

When implementing the unit, it is recommended that each model be presented in its entirety at least three times, with emphasis given to the literary analysis and rhetorical analysis models. Teachers are encouraged to use the complex features of the models, as these add depth and complexity to the unit content and encourage gifted students to think about the relationships between key ideas in more sophisticated ways. It is at the teacher's discretion to determine which model(s) are to be used for each lesson based upon students' interest, level of understanding, and engagement.

In-Class Activities to Deepen Learning

The activities included here provide hands-on or thought-provoking ideas that support or solidify student learning. Tasks incorporate real-world connections and include issue-based questions linked to a big idea, quick debates about a controversial issue, or technology extensions. These activities also include opportunities for self-reflection on how the lesson content impacted their learning. One or all of the activities in this section may be taught.

Concept Connections

The concept connections section focuses on the third component of the ICM. The purpose of this section is to help students see the relationships between different texts and perspectives as these relate to key generalizations about individuality versus conformity. A graphic organizer comprised of the conceptual generalizations and key unit readings is provided in the unit to help students organize their ideas and determine patterns among the various readings. It is important to refer to the concept generalizations in each lesson, even if the concept chart is not completed for every reading.

Choice-Based Differentiated Products

Several choice-based differentiated products are also part of each lesson. Students may select one of the choice products to showcase their strengths and individual understanding or, if pressed for time, teachers may require two or three choice-based products for students to complete during the course of the unit. The options listed allow students an opportunity to pursue their interests and to gain a deeper understanding of a learning objective as they present their understanding in a creative way. Differentiated products vary by lesson and may include investigating a real-world problem, designing visuals, applying an advanced model to other related sources, writing essays, and developing products or presentations for an audience. Rubrics are provided in Appendix C to guide product creation and teacher feedback. The rubrics may also be used for peer and self-evaluations.

ELA Practice Tasks

Designed with the CCSS assessments in mind, the ELA practice tasks support the writing and argument analysis items typically assessed as part of a state assessment. The ELA tasks incorporate multiple standards and require complex thinking. Students are asked to respond to a prompt by creating a well-developed essay in which they create or analyze arguments, critique texts, explain an issue from multiple perspectives, or explain the development of key concepts presented in a text. It is at the teacher's discretion to determine how many ELA practice tasks students should write throughout the course of the unit. Although not explicitly stated in the unit, teachers are encouraged to model the writing process, help students analyze exemplars and inappropriate responses, and provide individual feedback.

Formative Assessment

The formative assessment section focuses on assessing a student's understanding of a single-faceted objective such as making inferences or determining how an author used a literary element to convey an idea or theme. A rubric is included with each prompt so that teachers can quickly assess responses, provide feedback, and determine next steps in their students' learning. Questions require a written response of no more than a paragraph. The formative assessments may be used to determine the extent to which students understand the meaning of a text and can provide supporting evidence and target instruction based on individual needs. Teachers may require students to complete an ELA practice task in one lesson and a formative assessment task in another so that students' thinking and understanding can be measured in a variety of ways.

Handouts

Following each lesson, all necessary handouts for lesson completion are included (e.g., readings, visuals, organizers, blank analysis models, and other sources not readily available online). As previously stated in the materials section, sometimes teachers are led to specific web-based links or it is recommended that popular sources be found online. This is especially important for featured art (which doesn't copy well) and popularized primary sources and texts. Any source that is essential to the lesson or is difficult to access is included as a handout.

Other Unit Features

This unit includes a culminating lesson that synthesizes many of the learning objectives into a comprehensive project so that students may showcase their learning in a creative way. These options may include the application of the advanced content learned throughout the unit, real-world problem solving, and the development of authentic products. Additionally, the culminating lesson includes in-depth self-reflections that guide students to relate their own lives to concept-themes.

8

Rubrics are provided so that students understand the expectations of a task and teachers can easily analyze student products given set criteria. The rubrics are also useful for peer and self-evaluations.

Teacher background information is another feature found in many lessons, especially those with more complicated texts. Although some background information is provided, teachers are encouraged to study specific literary analysis critiques for a particular reading, research the history of a specific primary source (if not already known), and seek varied interpretations of the text or visual. Online links to literary critiques are provided for some lessons, when appropriate.

Sample responses are also included for many complex questions and analysis models. It is important to understand that the answers provided are a guide and should not be construed as the only correct response. Student answers will vary and many unanticipated responses may be correct. Teachers are encouraged to use the provided answers to better understand the intent of the question, to model how to arrive at an appropriate response, to demonstrate how to use a specific analysis model, and to familiarize themselves with the intent of a particular passage.

Finally, this unit features instructions for using models, sample lessons, blank model handouts, and guides to support students' thinking about each element of a given analysis model. Rubrics are also provided to assess student products and responses. Specifically, Appendix A highlights instructions, handouts, and examples for each analysis model. Appendix B includes blank models and guides for thinking about each element of a particular model, and Appendix C includes rubrics for assessing student progress.

Time Allotment

Most lessons can be taught within 90–120 minutes, although some lessons may take longer. The length of the lesson also depends upon how many models and activities are employed, how interested students are in a particular issue or text, and how many times a text needs to be read or analyzed for students to gain understanding. In general, it is anticipated that this unit can be taught with approximately 45 hours of instruction time if teachers follow the recommended guidelines as reported in this section.

Differentiation

Gifted students are a heterogeneous group and their ability levels, pace of learning, interests, and depth of understanding vary. Although this unit was written with gifted middle school students in mind, differentiation is still necessary. A variety of differentiated opportunities are embedded in the unit, such as choice-based product options, open-ended questions, and more simple and complex ways to adapt the analysis models and adjust instruction based on students' readiness and interest levels.

The "choice-based differentiated products" section in each lesson allows students to select a task of interest and to showcase their learning in a way that best meets their individual preferences and learning styles. In addition, the final lesson synthesizes unit goals and provides opportunities for students to select a project of their own choosing to explore in depth. The close reading questions can also be differentiated. Teachers may assign specific questions to individual students or groups of students based on their responses from formative assessments or ELA tasks.

The ELA process models (e.g., literary analysis, rhetorical analysis, and big idea reflection) are easily differentiated as well. For example, the literary and rhetorical analysis wheels automatically provide a framework for teachers to ask simple questions using only one element, or more complex questions by emphasizing relationships among various elements (e.g., how setting influences conflict, how figurative language contributes to characterization). Examples of simple and complex questions are included in selected lessons and also in Appendix A. Likewise, students who need more practice understanding a text may use the simpler text-based model (also in Appendix A) instead of the rhetorical analysis model. The teacher may also differentiate the in-class activities by assigning different groups of students to specific tasks. These can be designed as differentiated stations. Of course not all students would complete work at every station but would be assigned a station based on their readiness. After the complexity of the task is established, then activities, questions, or product choices are incorporated to accommodate various learning styles or interests.

The positive academic effects of grouping gifted students and accelerating the content they are taught are well documented (see the meta analyses of Kulik & Kulik, 1992, and Rogers, 2007). However, not all middle schools are designed to support accelerated courses for their high-achieving students. Experienced teachers of general classrooms may use this unit with their gifted and high-achieving students as part of a deliberate differentiated approach that includes in-class flexible groupings and tiered questions, stations, and assignments.

Multicultural Connections

Efforts were made to include sources that showcase a variety of authors from varying ethnicities, perspectives, and genders. Activities and readings encourage conversations about belongingness, questioning the status quo, and other key issues as these relate to individuality versus conformity. Teachers may substitute certain readings or adjust questions and discussions based on their specific school population and local community culture.

10

ASSESSMENT AND GRADING

Formative, diagnostic-prescriptive, and summative performance-based assessments are an essential part of the unit. Assessment data come from a variety of sources and are used to monitor student growth, provide student feedback, allow for student self-reflection, or to differentiate content or instruction. Descriptions of the assessments used in this unit are as follows:

- **Diagnostic-prescriptive assessment:** The unit pretest provides a first glimpse of a student's current level of performance. Each question focuses on a different key understanding. For example, Question 1 focuses on the relationship between different literary elements, Question 2 focuses on making inferences and providing evidence, and Question 3 focuses on concepts or themes. Reponses for each question can be used to differentiate questions for different groups of students and to assign specific tasks that support student learning in a key area. Prior to Lesson 1, administer the pretest (p. 14) and use the rubric (p. 16) to score responses.

- **Formative assessment:** There are many opportunities throughout the unit for teachers to check for student understanding. Teachers may occasionally ask students to expand, in writing, upon their answer to an assigned question from the text-dependent questions of a particular lesson so that comprehension can be assessed. A rubric is provided as part of the Formative Assessment section in each lesson to check for understanding. This rubric can also be used to monitor student growth and to provide feedback. The ELA Practice Tasks and Formative Assessment sections may also be assigned and graded to determine the level of student understanding as well as misconceptions about specific sources or texts that may need reteaching or further exploration. It is not recommended that every lesson's formative assessment or ELA task be assigned or graded, although teachers may select two or three of each throughout the course of the unit to use for this purpose. Informally, teachers may gather formative assessment data by listening to student discussions to ensure that students understand the text. Differentiated choice products may also be used as a formative assessment and graded using the provided rubric. Teachers should encourage students to engage in self-reflection as they receive feedback from a variety of assessments.

- **Summative assessment:** There are two different summative assessments in the unit. The final lesson (Lesson 12) includes culminating choice-based products for students to showcase their understanding of key unit content, processes, and concepts through selected product-creations. In addition, the postassessment of the unit can also be used as a summative assessment and also to measure student growth, when compared with the preassessment.

EVIDENCE SUPPORT FOR THE UNIT

Besides the use of an evidence-supported Conceptual Framework (ICM), this unit was piloted in a variety of classrooms middle school classrooms with either cluster grouped or homogeneous groups of gifted students. Teaching training was provided and teacher feedback was solicited regarding lesson clarity, student engagement, and the impact on student achievement and engagement. Lessons were modified as a result of teacher feedback and student responses. Pre- and postachievement data were also collected for this unit.

Students who were exposed to at least five lessons (almost half the unit) showed significant growth as evidenced by their pre-post-performance on the provided assessments. The unit preassessment was administered to students prior to teaching and the postassessment was administered upon conclusion of the unit. Trained individuals who had no association with writing or teaching the units scored the assessments. Students ($N = 120$) made statistically significant pretest ($M = 1.61$, $SD = .398$) to posttest ($M = 2.33$, $SD = .547$) gains [$t(17.157)$ $p = .000$] with important academic effects ($d = 1.64$) after correcting for dependence (see Morris & DeShon, 2002). This descriptive data suggest that after exposure to five or more lessons, students increase significantly in their ability to provide evidence or reasoning, justify a specific concept or idea, make inferences, and analyze specific literary elements.

Anecdotally, teachers reported that their students were more likely to notice connections among key ideas, concepts, literary and rhetorical elements, and multiple texts than before the unit was taught. In addition, their students discussed topics at a deeper level and offered more insights. They also liked that "teaching complexity was made easy" when using the unit's analysis models (e.g., literary analysis, rhetorical analysis) and as a result they were more confident that they were meeting the needs of their gifted learners than before unit implementation.

MAKING THE MOST OUT OF THE UNIT

The following ideas are important to consider before teaching the unit:
- Provide professional development about the units that includes both content and pedagogy. Some of the unit content is complex and background knowledge may be needed. Read Appendix A instructions and examples for using the analysis models before teaching the unit. Practice completing the models on your own using specific texts before asking the students to do so until you understand how the models are used.

12

For those students who need more scaffolding, consider teaching the models separately first with easier texts to get students accustomed to different ways of thinking before adding complex resources, issues, and concepts.

You may need to teach the individual elements of each analysis model before combining them. Still, it isn't necessary to teach an entire unit on mood or tone, for example, before using the literary analysis model, although students may need explanations and practice applying the individual elements first if they haven't been exposed prior. Because gifted students learn at a faster pace, teaching individual elements can be done more quickly so that you can focus on depth and complexity through the relationships between the different elements. (This concept applies to each of the models.)

Ensure that each individual lesson incorporates advanced content, an analysis model (e.g., literary, visual, or rhetorical), and links to the concept generalizations, as these are critical components of the ICM framework.

Read the texts and prompts ahead of time to make sure the selections are appropriate for your district context. Substitute readings and visuals as appropriate.

Consider informing parents of the unit contents and potentially controversial literature selections, concept discussions, and hot topics.

Make sure the online resources and YouTube videos are still available before teaching a particular lesson.

Follow your students. Sometimes a lesson or reading may prompt important discussions that continue beyond the allotted time period.

Know the intent of the models and the lesson outcomes so that you can best guide students toward important process, content, and concept goals. Otherwise, the issues discussed may supersede the objectives, especially with passionate gifted students.

Don't assign text-dependent questions as in-depth writing activities or homework as the norm. Discussion and teacher feedback are important and most of the questions in the unit are intended to be part of a small- or whole-group discussion. By engaging students through group discussions, you can correct misconceptions right away and solicit multiple perspectives and ideas that can enhance student learning.

Be sure to emphasize the use of supporting evidence and the complex relationships among various elements of a model when facilitating student discussions.

Have fun! We have enjoyed teaching these units and listening to teacher feedback. We hope these units not only show academic gains in your students but also encourage them to become citizens who can critically analyze situations and enact positive change.

UNIT GOALS AND OBJECTIVES

Content

Goal 1: To analyze and interpret texts and art. Students will be able to:
- explain with evidence how literary and/or visual elements contribute to the overall meaning of a work,
- explain with evidence how a writer supports a claim,
- respond to interpretations of texts through a variety of contexts by justifying ideas and providing new information,
- compare and contrast texts and real-world events on theme, and
- evaluate rhetoric within primary sources.

Process

Goal 2: To develop thinking, writing, and communication skills. Students will be able to:
- reason through an issue by analyzing points of view, assumptions, and implications;
- use evidence to develop and support inferences;
- evaluate the use of effective argumentation; and
- analyze societal or individual conflicts resulting from the struggle between individuality versus conformity.

Concept

Goal 3: To understand the concept of individuality versus conformity in the language arts. Students will be able to:
- support conformity versus individuality generalizations with evidence,
- develop and apply generalizations of additional key concepts, and
- explain the conflict between of conformity and individuality.

Pretest

"The Parable of the Poisoned Well" *by Author Unknown*

Directions: Read the text and write your responses to the questions below citing evidence from the text. After reading, complete the questions within 30 minutes.

There was once a wise king who ruled over a vast city. He was feared for his might and loved for his wisdom. Now in the heart of the city, there was a well whose waters were pure and crystalline from which the king and all the inhabitants drank. When all were asleep, an enemy entered the city and poured seven drops of a strange liquid into the well. And he said that henceforth all who drink this water shall become mad.

All the people drank of the water, but not the king. And the people began to say, "The king is mad and has lost his reason. Look how strangely he behaves. We cannot be ruled by a madman, so he must be dethroned."

The king grew very fearful, for his subjects were preparing to rise against him. So one evening, he ordered a golden goblet to be filled from the well, and he drank deeply. The next day, there was great rejoicing among the people, for their beloved king had finally regained his reason.

DOI: 10.4324/9781003235620-2

QUESTIONS

1. How does the author's use of literary techniques (e.g., point of view, conflict, plot, language, symbolism, characterization, setting, etc.) contribute to the overall meaning of the passage?

2. "The king grew very fearful, for his subjects were preparing to rise against him. So one evening, he ordered a golden goblet to be filled from the well, and he drank deeply." What inferences can be made about the king's motivation and conflict?

3. What does this story suggest about individuality versus conformity?

Pretest Rubric

"The Parable of the Poisoned Well" *by Author Unknown*

	0	1	2	3	4
Question 1: Content: Literary Analysis	Provides no response.	Response is limited and vague. There is no connection to how literary elements contribute to the meaning, main idea, or theme. A literary element is merely named.	Response is accurate with 1–2 literary techniques described with vague or no connection to a main idea or theme. Response includes limited or no evidence from text.	Response is appropriate and accurate, describing at least 2 literary elements and a main idea or theme. Response is literal and includes some evidence from the text.	Response is insightful and well supported, describing at least 2 literary elements and the theme. Response includes abstract connections and substantial evidence from the text.
Question 2: Inference From Evidence	Provides no response.	Response is limited, vague, and/or inaccurate. There is no justification for answers given.	Response is accurate, but lacks adequate explanation. Response includes some justification for either the character's motivation or conflict.	Response is accurate and makes sense. Response includes some justification about the character's motivation and conflict.	Response is accurate, insightful, interpretive, and well written. Response includes thoughtful justification about the character's motivation and conflict.
Question 3: Concept/ Theme	Provides no response.	Response is limited, vague, and/or inaccurate.	Response lacks adequate explanation. Response does not relate or create a generalization about individuality versus conformity. Little or no evidence from text.	Response is accurate and makes sense. Response relates to or creates an idea about individuality versus conformity with some relation to the text.	Response is accurate, insightful, and well written. Response relates to or creates a generalization about individuality versus conformity with evidence from the text.

Note: Adapted from *Jacob's Ladder Reading Comprehension Program: Level 4* (p. 148) by T. Stambaugh & J. VanTassel-Baska, 2001, New York, NY: Taylor & Francis. Copyright 2001 by Taylor & Francis. Adapted with permission.

I, Me, You, We © Taylor & Francis   DOI: 10.4324/9781003235620-3

AN EXAMINATION OF IDENTITY

How Does Our Environment Shape Our Identity?

DOI: 10.4324/9781003235620-4

Lesson

1

"Dark They Were and Golden-Eyed"
by Ray Bradbury

Goals/Objectives

Content: To analyze and interpret texts and art, students will be able to:
- explain with evidence how literary and/or visual elements contribute to the overall meaning of a work;
- respond to interpretations of texts through a variety of contexts by justifying ideas and providing new information; and
- compare and contrast texts and real-world events on theme.

Process: To develop thinking, writing, and communication skills, students will be able to:
- use evidence to develop appropriate inferences, and
- analyze societal or individual conflicts resulting from the struggle between individuality versus conformity.

Concept: To understand the concept of individuality versus conformity in the language arts, students will be able to:
- support conformity versus individuality generalizations with evidence,
- develop and apply generalizations of additional key concepts, and
- explain the conflict between conformity and individuality.

Accelerated CCSS ELA Standards

- RL.9-10.1
- RL.9-10.2
- RL.9-10.3
- RL.9-10.4
- RL.9-10.5
- SL.9-10.1
- SL.9-10.1c
- SL.9-10.1d

- W.9-10.4

 DOI: 10.4324/9781003235620-5

Materials

- Student copies of "Dark They Were and Golden Eyed" by Ray Bradbury, available at http://www.olgcnj.org/school/files/2010/10/E1006_dark_they_were_and_golden_eyed-4.pdf
- Butcher paper for groups of 3–4 and markers for each group
- Handout 1.1: Blank Literary Analysis Wheel
- Handout 1.2: Big Idea Reflection
- Handout 1.3: Concept Organizer
- Rubric 1: Product Rubric (Appendix C)

Introductory Activities

1. Distribute butcher paper to groups of 3–4 students and ask them to draw the concept of *conformity*. Leave the task open-ended. They can draw symbols but no words. Groups can share their drawings with the class, explaining any symbols.
2. Ask the class to come to an agreement on a definition for conformity. Ask:
   - What is conformity?
   - What other words are related to conformity (e.g., change, loss of identity, etc.)?
   - Is conformity always negative?
   - In what situations is it beneficial to conform?
   - What is the opposite of conformity? Is individuality really the opposite?
   - How are these two concepts related?

3. Explain that this unit is about the conflict between conformity and individuality. In some lessons, this is about a unique individual conforming to group expectations, while in other lessons it is about being alone versus being with community. Some lessons will explore the benefits of challenging the status quo, while others explore the benefits of being a part of a majority. Students will be examining various works of art, literature, and nonfiction text to gain more insight into these concepts. Discuss or reflect in writing:
   - Why is conformity important to humans?
   - Why is it important to society?
   - When is it good? When is it bad?

4. Show several video clips from movies relating individuality versus conformity. Ask students to develop generalizations about individuality versus conformity after viewing the clips. Some suggestions include:
   - "Real You" from *Cloudy with a Chance of Meatballs*, available at http://www.wingclips.com/movie-clips/cloudy-with-a-chance-of-meatballs/real-you

- "A Little Different" from *Cloudy with a Chance of Meatballs*, available at http://www.wingclips.com/movie-clips/cloudy-with-a-chance-of-meatballs/a-little-different
- "Meeting the Giant" from *Big Fish*, available at http://www.wingclips.com/movie-clips/big-fish/meeting-the-giant
- "Fearless Despereaux" from *The Tale of Despereaux*, available at http://www.wingclips.com/movie-clips/tale-of-desperaux/fearless-desperaux

Examples of generalizations: *Individuality requires courage. Society's rules about conformity are designed to keep people safe.*

5. Briefly introduce the vocabulary words that students will encounter in this lesson. Students may develop a chart for these words (see Figure 1.1 for an example). You may wish to divide the words among students (giving them words they do not know) to look them up in the dictionary or an online source. Discuss meanings as they fill in the chart.
   - **Forlorn:** Lonely and miserable
   - **Recede:** To go back
   - **Villa:** A vacation house
   - **Convivial:** Pleasant, sociable
   - **Sapling:** A small tree
   - **Muse:** To gaze thoughtfully
   - **Bewildered:** Confused

Read Text

Distribute copies of "Dark They Were and Golden-Eyed." Conduct a version of reader's theater. Students will read assigned parts of the story aloud. (*Note:* Although the story is not written as a play, it can still be read in parts if the students are savvy about following along and understand the dialogue.) Assign the following parts:
- Narrator
- Harry Bittering
- Cora Bittering
- Tim
- Laura
- Dan
- Sam
- Simpson
- Lieutenant
- Captain
- Others: The men, the people

22

Word	Know	Think I Know	Don't Know	Meaning
Forlorn			X	
Recede				
Villa				
Convivial				
Sapling				
Muse				
Bewildered				

Figure 1.1. Sample vocabulary chart.

Text-Dependent Questions

Select from the following questions for leading a Socratic seminar or class discussion:

- What patterns do you notice about grass and bone in the first few paragraphs? Why might Bradbury use this imagery? (Sample response: Both are contrasting ideas. Grass can refer to growth; bones are associated with death. Both will be important foreshadowing devices to the theme—death of old identity, birth of new.)
- "One day the atom bomb will fix Earth, then we'll be safe here." Why do you think they are on Mars? (Sample response: To escape the Atomic War.)
- Re-read the paragraph beginning with "Alone, thought Bittering . . . ." What does this reveal about Bittering's character? (Sample response: His actions are not in line with his thoughts.)
- "Nevertheless, man lives by symbol and label." What point is Bradbury making? (Sample response: Identities or names are given to the Martian hills, but these names change depending on who names them. This foreshadows the changing of identity for Bittering later in the story.)
- Notice Bradbury's style in writing "You know they have! Onions, but not onions, carrots, but not carrots . . . ." Why does Bradbury use this style and what effect does it have on the story? (Sample response: It shows that there is something slightly different about their nature, and this may allude to the big idea of the story.)
- Why does Bradbury choose "autumn" to be the season to work on the rocket? (Sample response: Autumn may symbolize change, and students should refer to other textual evidence that the story emphasizes change.)
- What is significant about the rusting rocket? (Sample response: His identity/dreams are rusting away.) What is significant about the broken mirror?

(Sample response: Shattered identity.) Do you notice any other symbols? (Sample response: Changing eye color = changing perspective.)

- Which character most influences Bittering's change?
- How does Bradbury develop and contrast character perspectives?
- Is Sam a necessary character in the story? How would the story's theme development be different without him?
- What is Bradbury's purpose in writing this text? How do you know?
- What specific quotes best support the theme of the story?

Literary Analysis

1. Guide students through a literary analysis using Handout 1.1: Blank Literary Analysis Wheel. Lead students through a basic discussion of each literary element, then emphasize the interaction of the elements with more complex questions. Note the inner wheel conceptually spins so that its elements interact with each other and the outer wheel. Refer to Literary Analysis Instructions (Appendix A) for detailed instructions about the Blank Literary Analysis Wheel and how to make a hands-on model. Encourage students to cite textual evidence throughout discussion. The Literary Analysis Wheel Guide (Appendix B) shows specific concepts for each element of the wheel. They may take notes on the Blank Literary Analysis Wheel using arrows to show how elements relate. Consider making a poster of the Literary Analysis Wheel Guide to refer to throughout the unit.

2. Focus on the following complex questions:
   - How does Bradbury's use of language descriptions about the setting affect the mood of the story?
   - How do plot elements enhance the mood and suspense?
   - How does Bradbury use conflict to reveal character motives and values?
   - How do symbols enhance the theme?
   - How does point of view affect the theme? How would the story be different if told from Mrs. Bittering's point of view? What other elements would be different?

3. The following notes may be helpful in guiding students through the analysis:
   - **Themes:** Themes relate to fear, change of identity, and label.
   - **Symbols:** Rusting rocket = rusting away of identity; mirror breaking = identity breaking; eyes changing color = perspectives of life changing, autumn = change. Consider elements of foreshadowing as referred to in the text-dependent questions (bone/grass, symbol/label of mountains = new identities).

Context: This story was written in 1949 with the original title of "Naming of Names." How might the time period be influential on this piece? (Consider the end of WWII.)

Big Idea Reflection

(Optional) Use Handout 1.2: Big Idea Reflection for relating the text to real life.
- **Concepts:** Identity, change, environment, home, individual, society, dreams, goals.
- **Generalizations:** Where you are can change who you are.
- **Issue/Problem:** Person versus society; to conform or not conform.
- **Insight:** Change is influenced by multiple factors including environment and people. Just as Bittering was determined to make a rocket, but soon abandoned his focus, we can be distracted in pursuing our own goals.
- **World/Community/Individual:** Individual—Do my values change subtly? What's influencing me? How does "where I am" affect "who I am"?
- **Solution/Implications:** How might I respond to the pressures to conform? What are the implications on my life if I change as a result of the influences around me?

In-Class Activities to Deepen Learning

1. **Engage students in a quick debate.** Originally this story was published as "The Naming of Names." Ask: *Which is a more appropriate title and why? Support your answer with textual evidence. Consider symbolism.* Students may stand on opposite sides of the room to defend their answers.
2. Ask students to develop a skit portraying what happened right before the story begins or what happens right after the story ends. Within their skit, they should relate to the idea of individuality or conformity.

Concept Connections

1. Explain to students that during the unit, they will be looking at specific concepts related to the theme of conformity versus individuality. Ask: *What general statements can we say about conformity and individuality? We will call these general statements "generalizations" because we can take an idea from a specific work and generalize it to the broader world.*
2. Explain that in this unit, they will focus on three major generalizations related to the concept/theme of conformity versus individuality. They are:
   - Both conformity and individuality are agents of change.
   - Both conformity and individuality involve sacrifice.

◦ There are positives and negatives to both conformity and individuality.

Consider displaying the generalizations on a poster to be referred to throughout the unit. Lead students through a discussion using Handout 1.3: Concept Organizer. Students can record their thoughts in future lessons to see how various works compare and contrast.

3. Students should list examples about how the work demonstrates some of these generalizations in the first column of the concept organizer. Provide guidance as needed. Ask: *How are these generalizations exemplified in the text? Are there other generalizations we can make about conformity from this text?* Ask students to also develop a generalization noting the relationship between conformity/individuality and another concept (e.g., identity, freedom, power, acceptance). The sentence should be relevant to the text. Tell students they will continue to add to this chart in future lessons. Figure 1.2 provides some sample responses.

Choice-Based Differentiated Products

Students may choose one of the following independent products to complete (*Note*: Use Rubric 1: Product Rubric in Appendix C to assess student products):

◦ Rewrite the story as if Mr. Bittering did not lose his identity and maintained his identity as an Earthling. Consider how this change in the plot might affect the mood and evoke other conflicts. Carefully consider your word choice as you develop your narrative.

◦ Consider how the setting affected Mr. Bittering's loss of identity. Relate this situation to a real-life contemporary issue. Does where we are change who we are? Write a few paragraphs explaining how you notice this in the real world in at least three ways.

◦ Choose a song that relates to the theme(s) in the story. Write at least three ways the story is similar to the song. Be sure to cite textual evidence from the story as well as specific reference to song lyrics (at least three lyric lines).

◦ Choose the 20 most powerful descriptive words or phrases from the story. Then, create your own original poem with these words to describe the idea of changing one's identity.

ELA Practice Tasks

Assign one of the following tasks as a performance-based assessment for this lesson:

◦ In an essay, describe how Bradbury's word choice about the setting affects the mood of the story. Include reference to specific words and phrases

Both conformity and individuality are agents of change.
Bittering's conforming to Martian culture involved a change in his identity.
Both conformity and individuality involve sacrifice.
Bittering sacrificed his own dreams as he evolved into a Martian.
There are positives and negatives to both conformity and individuality.
Bittering's conformity allowed him to let go of worry while being with his family; however, he lost his own dreams.
Examine the relationship between conformity, individuality, and another related concept.
Conformity involves losing part of one's identity and gaining acceptance.

Figure 1.2. *How are these generalizations exemplified in the text? Are there other generalizations we can make about conformity from this text?* Sample responses.

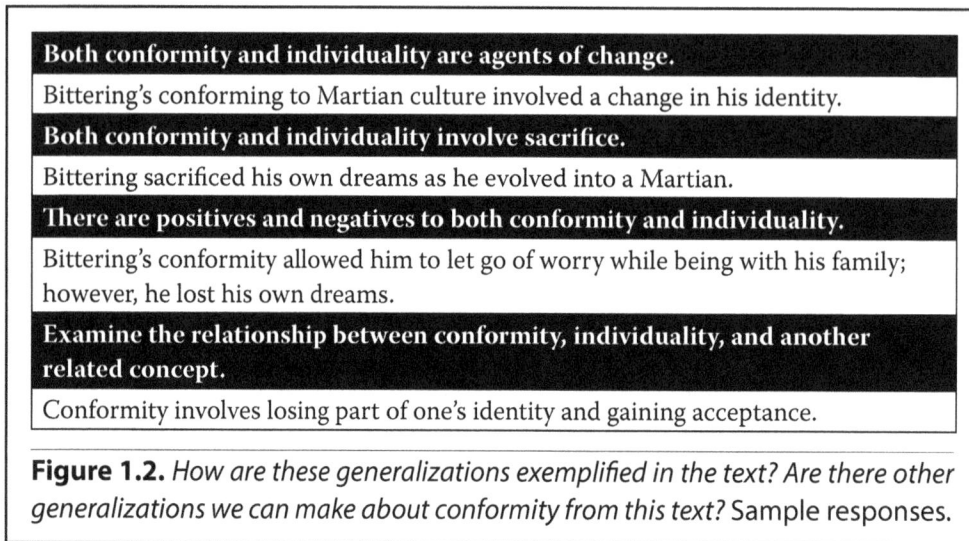

throughout the entire plot. Consider how the mood changes through the plot.

- How does Bradbury use symbols to reveal the theme of individuality versus conformity in the story? Explain your answer in a well-developed essay citing sufficient evidence from the text.
- How does Bittering change throughout the story? Consider causes and effects of his change. Cite sufficient textual evidence to support your answer in an explanatory essay.

Formative Assessment

1. Ask students to respond to the following prompt in a single paragraph: *What does this story reveal about individuality versus conformity? Be sure to refer to a generalization in your response.*
2. Use the scoring guidelines in Figure 1.3 to evaluate students' responses.

	Concept/Theme
0	Provides no response.
1	Response is limited, vague, and/or inaccurate.
2	Response lacks adequate explanation. Response does not relate or create a generalization about individuality versus conformity. Little or no evidence from text.
3	Response is accurate and makes sense. Response relates to or creates an idea about individuality versus conformity with some relation to the text.
4	Response is accurate, insightful, and well written. Response relates to or creates a generalization about individuality versus conformity with evidence from the text.

Figure 1.3. Scoring guidelines for Lesson 1 formative assessment.

Handout 1.1
Blank Literary Analysis Wheel

Directions: Draw arrows across elements to show connections.

Text: _____

Purpose/Context

Setting

Mood

Symbols

Language
Structure
Style

Plot/
Conflict

Characters

Theme

Point of View

Tone

Interpretation

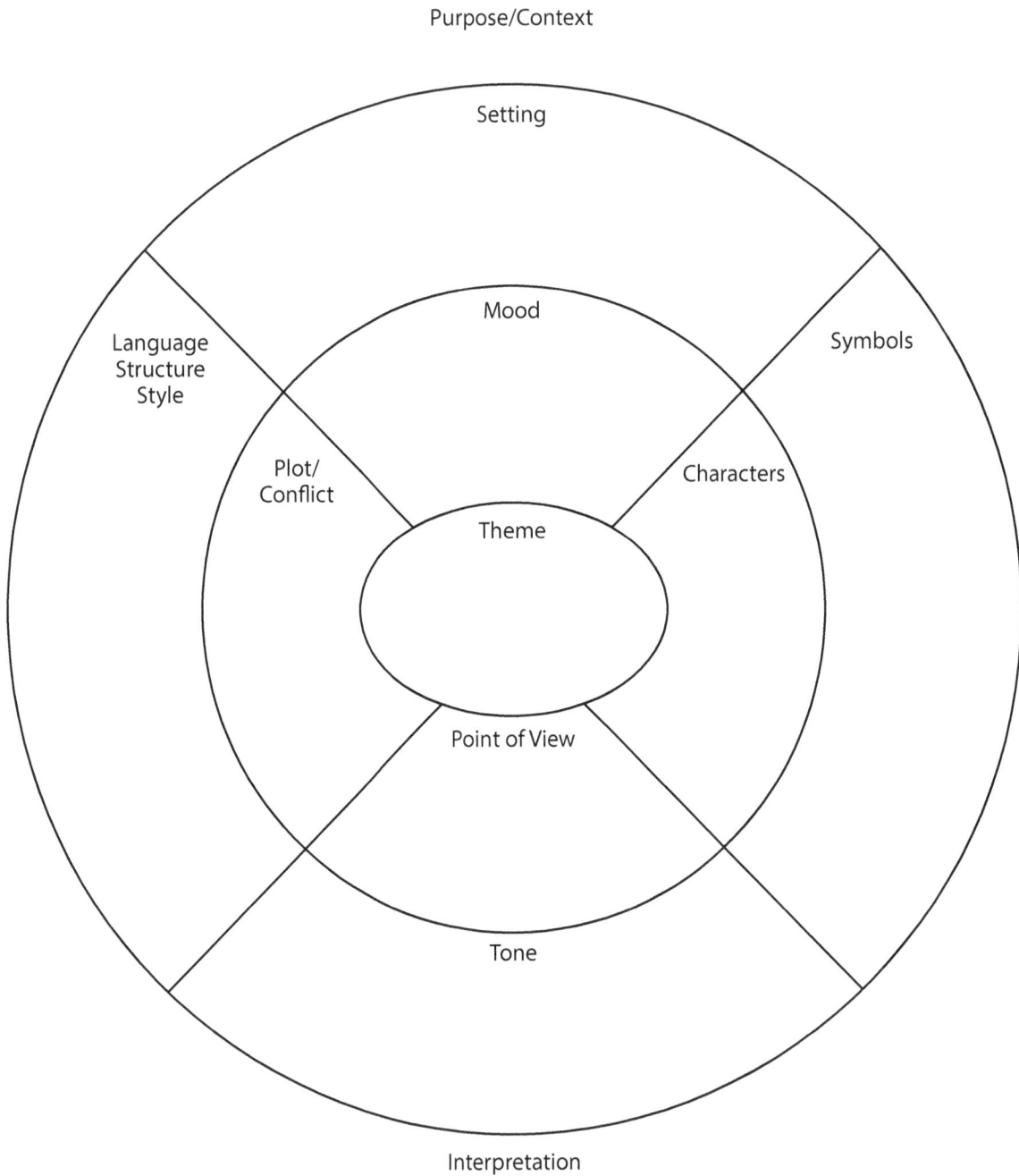

Created by Tamra Stambaugh, Ph.D., & Emily Mofield, Ed.D., 2015.

Name: _____ Date: _____

Handout 1.2
Big Idea Reflection

<table>
<tr>
<td rowspan="3">What?</td>
<td>Concepts:
What concepts/ideas are in the text?</td>
<td></td>
</tr>
<tr>
<td>Generalizations:
What broad statement can you make about one or more of these concepts? Make it generalizable beyond the text.</td>
<td></td>
</tr>
<tr>
<td>Issue:
What is the main issue, problem, or conflict?</td>
<td></td>
</tr>
<tr>
<td rowspan="2">So What?</td>
<td>Insight:
What insight on life is provided from this text?</td>
<td></td>
</tr>
<tr>
<td>World/Community/Individual:
How does this text relate to you, your community, or your world? What question does the author want you to ask yourself?</td>
<td></td>
</tr>
<tr>
<td>Now What?</td>
<td>Implications:
How should you respond to the ideas in the text? What action should you take? What are the implications of the text? What can you do with this information?</td>
<td></td>
</tr>
</table>

Created by Emily Mofield, Ed.D., & Tamra Stambaugh, Ph.D., 2015.

Handout 1.3
Concept Organizer

Directions: How does each work exemplify each generalization? What new generalization can you make?

Literature, Art, or Media: _____	Literature, Art, or Media: _____	Literature, Art, or Media: _____
Both conformity and individuality are agents of change.		
Both conformity and individuality involve sacrifice.		
There are positives and negatives to both conformity and individuality.		
Examine the relationship between conformity and/or individuality and another concept.		

This page intentionally left blank.

Lesson

2

"All Summer in a Day"
by Ray Bradbury

Goals/Objectives

Content: To analyze and interpret texts and art, students will be able to:

- explain with evidence how literary and/or visual elements contribute to the overall meaning of a work,
- respond to interpretations of texts through a variety of contexts by justifying ideas and providing new information, and
- compare and contrast texts and real-world events on theme.

Process: To develop thinking, writing, and communication skills, students will be able to:

- use evidence to develop appropriate inferences, and
- analyze societal or individual conflicts resulting from the struggle between individuality versus conformity.

Concept: To understand the concept of individuality versus conformity in the language arts, students will be able to:

- support conformity versus individuality generalizations with evidence,
- develop and apply generalizations of additional key concepts, and
- explain the conflict between conformity and individuality.

Accelerated CCSS ELA Standards

- RL.9-10.1
- RL.9-10.2
- RL.9-10.3
- RL.9-10.4
- RL.9-10.5
- SL.9-10.1
- SL.9-10.1c
- SL.9-10.1d
- SL.9-10.4
- W.9-10.4

DOI: 10.4324/9781003235620-6

Materials

- Student copies of "All Summer in a Day" by Ray Bradbury, available at http://www.btboces.org/Downloads/6_All%20Summer%20in%20a%20 Day%20by%20Ray%20Bradbury.pdf
- (Optional) Handout 1.3: Concept Organizer
- Handout 2.1: Blank Literary Analysis Wheel
- Handout 2.2: Big Idea Reflection
- Rubric 1: Product Rubric (Appendix C)

Introductory Activities

1. Ask students to respond to the following descriptive writing prompt: *How would you describe sunshine to someone who never experienced it? Include similes, metaphors, and other figurative language in your description.*
2. Play a quick game of "Would You Rather" to get students to start thinking about the story they are about to read. Ask: *Would you rather be right about something but no one believe you, or be wrong about something and everyone believe you?*
3. Preteach the following vocabulary words:
   - **Vital:** Extremely important
   - **Tumultuous:** Unrestrained
   - **Slacken:** To become less intense
   - **Resilient:** Able to recover quickly

Read Text

Distribute copies of "All Summer in a Day." Students may read the text independently or you may conduct a scaled-down version of reader's theater. Do this by assigning the following parts. Students will read those parts of the story aloud. (*Note:* Although the story is not written as a play, it can still be read in parts if the students are savvy about following along and understand the dialogue.)

- Narrator
- Children (the text starts with various children)
- Margot
- William
- Teacher

Text-Dependent Questions

Select from the following questions for leading a Socratic seminar or class discussion:

- How does Margot describe the sun? Why are these descriptions important to the story? How does it enhance our understanding of her character?
- In what ways is Margot different from the children? Keep a chart of textual evidence.
- How does the setting affect the conflict between Margot and the other children?
- What does Margot's shower experience tell us about her ability to cope on Venus?
- What is significant about the following simile: "They stood as if someone had driven them, like so many stakes, into the floor"?
- Did the sun change the children? According to the text, did the children change for the better? How might the sun represent a more abstract idea/meaning? (Sample response: The sun represents bringing them into the light of truth.)
- How does Bradbury use "white" imagery to describe Margot? (Sample response: Whitened, pale, snow.) Why might he do this? What could this symbolize? How does he use "white" imagery to describe the children at the end? (Sample response: They are referred to as pale.) In what ways might this be significant? (Sample response: The white imagery is indicative of Margot's innocence and "purity" as a character. She is the "enlightened" one in the story who knows the truth. In the end, the children are also "enlightened" with truth.)
- What part of the story is most indicative of Margot's character?
- How will Margot respond to the children after the story is over? Will it be a positive or negative reaction? Use evidence from the text about her character to support your hypothesis.
- What is the theme of the story? What specific quotes support the story's theme?

Literary Analysis

1. Guide students through a literary analysis using Handout 2.1: Blank Literary Analysis Wheel. Lead students through a basic discussion of each literary element, then emphasize the interaction of the elements with more complex questions. Encourage students to cite textual evidence throughout discussion. Students can take notes on the wheel and draw arrows to illustrate connections between concepts.

2. Focus on the following complex questions:

How does setting contribute to the development of character? How is the setting symbolic of characters and conflict?

How would the theme of the story be different if Margot had not been locked in the closet?

How does Bradbury's characterization of Margot create conflict in the plot?

How does the point of view (third person limited) influence the mood of the story?

3. The following notes may be helpful in guiding students through the analysis:

Themes: Themes relate to bullying, being an outsider, loneliness, kids being jealous of someone with "superior" knowledge, people who are different/isolated.

Symbols: The sun may represent how the children were enlightened. The sun changed the children—they realized the truth and with this, they have regret about leaving Margot in the closet.

Setting /Symbols:

- The setting of the storm is a symbol of the storm within Margot. This is a "pathetic fallacy." This is a tool authors use to reveal characters' emotions through setting.
- The flesh-like weeds in the jungle may symbolize how the characters are "trapped" on Venus and also trapped in their way of thinking before seeing the truth of the sun.
- The ash jungle may represent the absence of "green" (life) just as the children lack a deep awareness of life like Margot.

Character/Symbols: The story is a universal story of the "enlightened one" having knowledge others do not have. This character tries to help others see the truth. The "enlightened" one is often ridiculed for his or her knowledge and associated with "white" imagery. Students may think of other stories with this pattern.

Context: This story was written in 1954, the precipice of space exploration.

Big Idea Reflection

Using Handout 2.2: Big Idea Reflection, relate the text to real life. This may be done in small groups or whole class discussion.

Concepts: Uniqueness, bullying, identity, enlightenment, regret, knowledge, truth, rejection.

- **Generalizations:** The "enlightened" one is often rejected by the majority.
- **Issue/Problem:** Bullying, being different, not being accepted.
- **Insight:** The enlightened ones are often ridiculed for claiming to know what others don't. Others are often jealous of those with superior knowledge.
- **World/Community/Individual:** Am I treated differently because I'm smart? Do I treat others unfairly?
- **Solution/Implications:** How might I personally respond to these problems in my world? What are the implications of these issues on my life?

In-Class Activities to Deepen Learning

1. **Engage students in a quick debate.** Ask: *Would it have been better for Margot to never have experienced the sun in her life? Did the children change for the better? How do you know (from the text)? Why or why not?* Students may argue their points of view by standing on opposite sides of the room.
2. Compare literary elements in "All Summer in a Day" with "Dark They Were and Golden-Eyed" on a chart. Help students understand that both involve ideas related to individuality (see Figure 2.1 for an example).
3. Ask students to develop three to four questions for Margot, William, and the students. In a talk-show format, ask students to perform interviews of the guests regarding why they act they way they do, how they feel throughout the story, and how they feel toward one another.
4. Develop a social/emotional connection for students. Ask: *Margot is shunned because others are jealous of her. Do you think other students are "jealous" of advanced learners/gifted students? Have you ever been shunned or ostracized because you have knowledge others do not have? What are healthy ways to cope with this? How does this compare to the story?*

Concept Connections

Discuss connections to individuality versus conformity by asking the following questions. Students may reflect on concept connections using Handout 1.3: Concept Organizer, continued from Lesson 1. Figure 2.2 provides some sample responses.

- What does this text reveal about the pros and cons of conformity?
- How did Margot experience the positive aspects of individuality?
- How is Margot's individuality an agent for change?
- What new generalizations about individuality or conformity can you make based on this story?

38

"Dark They Were and Golden-Eyed"	Comparisons	"All Summer in a Day"
Mars, physical changes affect their behavior (wind).	Setting: Both set on planets that affect the behavior of characters.	Venus, extreme weather affects behavior (rain).
Conflict spurred by changing motives of other characters (stay on Mars).	Conflict: Both experience a person versus society conflict.	Conflict spurred by jealousy.
Bittering first fights to be different, but then conforms.	Characters: Both display a struggle to maintain individuality/identity.	Margot is ostracized for her identity.
Change, identity, memory, conformity, dreams.	Themes: Both relate to individuality versus conformity and identity.	Bullying, jealousy, individuality, disbelief, ridicule, identity.
	Consider other elements (plot patterns, symbolism, etc.).	

Figure 2.1. Sample literary elements comparison chart.

Both conformity and individuality are agents of change.

Margot's individuality (uniqueness) caused others to dislike her; yet when others recognized the truth, they changed.

Both conformity and individuality involve sacrifice.

Margot was mistreated because of her individuality/uniqueness.

There are positives and negatives to both conformity and individuality.

Positive: Margot knew the truth about the sun and had memories no one else had. Negative: She was mistreated; no one believed her.

Examine the relationship between conformity, individuality, and another related concept.

Maintaining one's individuality (uniqueness) may lead to jealousy, oppression, or a loss of freedom.

Figure 2.2. Sample student responses to individuality versus conformity generalizations.

Choice-Based Differentiated Products

Students may choose one of the following independent products to complete (*Note*: Use Rubric 1: Product Rubric in Appendix C to assess student products):

- Write a dialogue between Margot from "All Summer in a Day" and Mr. Bittering from "Dark They Were and Golden-Eyed." In the dialogue, include at least three quotes from each story as they talk about their similar experiences relating to individuality/conformity.
- From the perspective of Margot, write a poem about sunshine using vivid imagery, similes, and metaphors. Write it to show Margot's unique perspective compared to her social peers.
- One theme from "All Summer in a Day" relates to the unintended consequences of bullying. Develop an antibullying campaign to address bullying at your school. Collect data on bullying instances at your school (ask permission from school administration), identify problem areas, and present an action plan for a solution. Present your action plan to your school leaders.

ELA Practice Tasks

Assign one of the following tasks as a performance-based assessment for this lesson:

- In a multiparagraph essay, compare and contrast Margot from "All Summer in a Day" to Mr. Bittering from "Dark They Were and Golden-Eyed." In your essay, use specific details from both works to support how these characters deal with the conflict of conformity versus individuality. Cite sufficient evidence from the text, including page numbers and direct quotes.
- Think about the details Bradbury used to develop Margot's character. Write a continuation of the story to pick up where the story ended. Consider whether Margot will respond positively or negatively to the children based on what you already know about her. Use dialogue, figurative language, and use of internal conflict as literary techniques in your narrative.

Formative Assessment

1. Ask students to respond to the following prompt in a single paragraph: *What can you infer about the boy's point of view in the following text? How does this relate to the central conflict in the text?*

	Inference From Evidence
0	Provides no response.
1	Response is limited, vague, and/or inaccurate. There is no justification for answers given.
2	Response is accurate, but lacks adequate explanation. Response includes some justification about the conflict.
3	Response is accurate and makes sense. Response includes some justification about the conflict.
4	Response is accurate, insightful, interpretive, and well written. Response includes thoughtful justification about the conflict.

Figure 2.3. Scoring guidelines for Lesson 2 formative assessment.

"Well, don't wait around here!" cried the boy savagely. "You won't see nothing!"

Her lips moved.

"Nothing!" he cried. "It was all a joke, wasn't it?" He turned to the other children. "Nothing's happening today. Is it?"

2. Use the scoring guidelines in Figure 2.3 to evaluate students' responses.

Name: _____ Date: _____

Handout 2.1
Blank Literary Analysis Wheel

Directions: Draw arrows across elements to show connections.

Text: _____

Purpose/Context

Setting

Mood

Language
Structure
Style

Symbols

Plot/
Conflict

Characters

Theme

Point of View

Tone

Interpretation

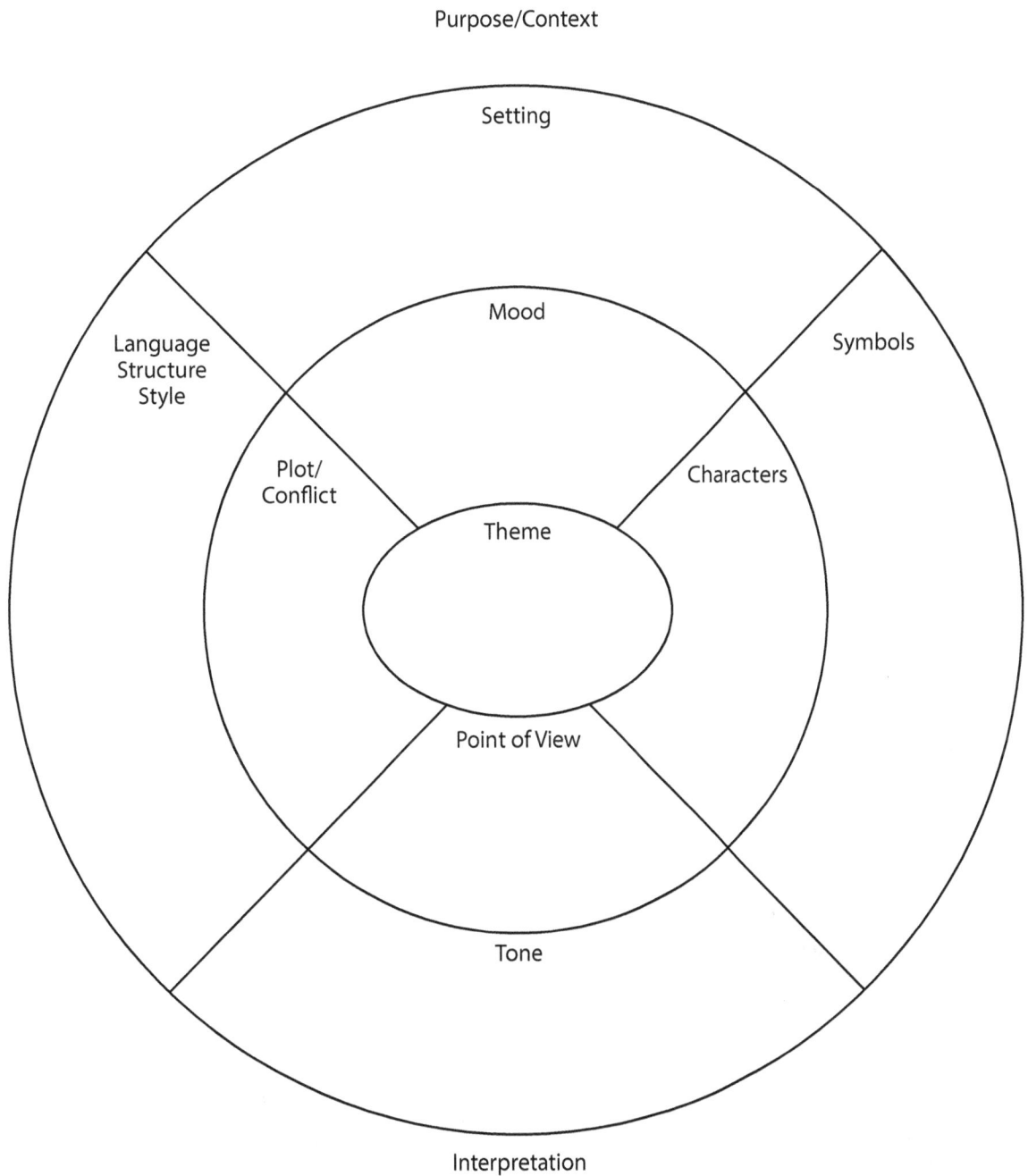

Created by Tamra Stambaugh, Ph.D., & Emily Mofield, Ed.D., 2015.

Name: _____ Date: _____

Handout 2.2
Big Idea Reflection

What?	**Concepts:** What concepts/ideas are in the text?	
	Generalizations: What broad statement can you make about one or more of these concepts? Make it generalizable beyond the text.	
	Issue: What is the main issue, problem, or conflict?	
So What?	**Insight:** What insight on life is provided from this text?	
	World/Community/Individual: How does this text relate to you, your community, or your world? What question does the author want you to ask yourself?	
Now What?	**Implications:** How should you respond to the ideas in the text? What action should you take? What are the implications of the text? What can you do with this information?	

Created by Emily Mofield, Ed.D., & Tamra Stambaugh, Ph.D., 2015.

This page intentionally left blank.

Lesson

3

"Day and Night"
by M. C. Escher

Goals/Objectives

Content: To analyze and interpret texts and art, students will be able to:
- explain with evidence how literary and/or visual elements contribute to the overall meaning of a work,
- respond to interpretations of texts through a variety of contexts by justifying ideas and providing new information, and
- compare and contrast texts and real-world events on theme.

Process: To develop thinking, writing, and communication skills, students will be able to:
- use evidence to develop and support inferences, and
- analyze societal or individual conflicts resulting from the struggle between individuality versus conformity.

Concept: To understand the concept of individuality versus conformity in the language arts, students will be able to:
- support conformity versus individuality generalizations with evidence,
- develop and apply generalizations of additional key concepts, and
- explain the conflict between conformity and individuality.

Accelerated ELA CCSS Standards

SL.8.2	SL.9-10.1c	W.9-10.4
SL.9-10.1	SL.9-10.1d	RI.9-10.7

Materials

- M. C. Escher's *Day and Night* to display, available online
- (Optional) Three or four Escher drawings to show whole class (e.g., *The Bridge, Drawing Hands*, and *Predestination*; available online)

 DOI: 10.4324/9781003235620-7

  * Handout 1.3: Concept Organizer
  * Handout 3.1: Blank Visual Analysis Wheel
  * Rubric 1: Product Rubric (Appendix C)

Introductory Activity

Ask students to each draw a picture to answer the question: *How does our environment shape our identity?* Have students discuss their sketches with peers. Ask: *Are we products of our surroundings? What influences change?*

View Art

1. Display M. C. Escher's *Day and Night* (or distribute student copies). Do not share the title yet or disclose any background information. Ask every student to respond in a round-robin response (no discussion yet) to the following statements. This will allow students to see various aspects of the art before analyzing it:
   * Say: *I see something you don't see.* Ask students to say one thing they see in the painting that they think others have difficulty seeing (i.e., "I see a windmill," I see a small bridge . . . ")
   * Ask: *What title would you give this piece of art? Why?* (Students may share with partner and then with the whole group.)

2. Reveal the title of the work: *Day and Night* by M. C. Escher (woodcut, 1938). Ask: *Why is the title meaningful?*
3. Give a brief background sketch on M. C. Escher (1898–1972). He is a famous 20th-century Dutch artist who is known for developing impossible structures within his art. He has made more than 448 lithographs (original prints) and woodcarvings, and more than 2,000 drawings. Escher also wrote many poems and essays, and he studied architecture, although he never graduated from high school. He used many mathematical aspects in his works. Most of Escher's works involve his own fascination with the concept of reality. His works showing paradoxes, tessellations, and impossible objects have influenced graphic art, psychology, philosophy, and logic.
4. Show a couple of his works (optional) to further expose students to his style, such as *The Bridge, Drawing Hands,* and *Predestination.* Ask students to note features of his style.

Visual Analysis

Discuss the painting using the framework of a visual analysis. Distribute Handout 3.1: Blank Visual Analysis Wheel. Lead students through a basic understanding of each element, then emphasize the interaction of the elements with more complex questions. Note the inner wheel conceptually spins so that its elements interact with each other and the outer wheel. Refer to Appendix A for detailed instructions about the Visual Analysis Wheel. The Visual Analysis Wheel Guide (Appendix B) shows specific prompts to guide students in thinking through each separate concept. They may take notes on the Blank Visual Analysis Wheel using arrows to show how concepts relate. The following questions and sample responses are a guide to help the teacher elicit responses through scaffolding; however multiple interpretations are encouraged as long as they are justified with evidence.

Context/Purpose:
- *What is the context of this work?* M. C. Escher made this woodcut in 1938.
- *What do you think his purpose/motive is in creating this?* Students may not grasp the purpose—to express ideas about setting and change—until the analysis is complete.

Point of View/Assumptions:
- *What is the artist's point of view about change?* Drastic change can happen gradually.

Images/Technique/Structure:
- **Images:** *What do you see first (e.g., black or white)? What are the main images? What could the images symbolize?* Consider black/white, birds, bridges. *Do the canals meet? At what place does the print seem to "move?"*
- **Technique:** *What technique does Escher use to show his ideas?* Tessellations, use of only black and white, use of symmetry, mirrored worlds. *Is it really symmetrical?*
- **Structure:** *What do you notice when you move your eyes from the bottom of the print to the top?* The block of plains turns into birds.

Emotions/Technique/Structure:
- *What emotions does this evoke in you? How did the artist accomplish this?* Students may consider a lack of emotion portrayed in the art. Sometimes we are unaware of how we change in response to where we are.

Artist Background/Technique/Structure:
- Review information provided in the lesson.

Main Idea:
- *What is the main idea in* Day and Night*?* Change—where you are changes who you are. The process of change is gradual.

Implications:
- *What are the implications of viewing this art?* It allows for personal reflection about how I am influenced by my surroundings.

Evaluation:
- *Do you like this art? Would you hang it in your home? Does it make you think? Was the artist successful in presenting his ideas? Justify your answers with evidence.*

In-Class Activities to Deepen Learning

Make connections. Ask:
- How does this piece of art reflect ideas related to "Dark They Were and Golden-Eyed"? (Perhaps students will see the idea of changing identity—the Earthlings changing to Martians. Where we are can change who we are, as reflected in both the text and art.)
- How does this piece of art reflect ideas related to "All Summer in a Day?" (Perhaps students will see connection of children going "into the light" and seeing for themselves the world that Margot knew existed all along, a world with the sun. The children were at one time in the dark, or ignorant. The experience of seeing the sun changed them, as they felt regret for leaving Margot in the closet.)

Concept Connections

Discuss connections to individuality versus conformity by asking the following questions. Students may reflect on concept connections using Handout 1.3: Concept Organizer, continued from previous lessons. Figure 3.1 provides some sample responses.
- How does the art reveal leaving behind part of your true self?
- What positive aspects of conformity are portrayed in the art?

| Both conformity and individuality are agents of change. |
| As the swans move from one place to another, they change identity; where we are can change who we are. |
| Both conformity and individuality involve sacrifice. |
| Changing to one's new environment involves losing part of your original identity. |
| There are positives and negatives to both conformity and individuality. |
| In conforming to be a part of a new environment, one can be comfortable, yet this involves leaving behind a part of your true self. |
| Examine the relationship between conformity, individuality, and another related concept. |
| Students may consider concepts of change, identity, freedom, and location. |

Figure 3.1. Sample student responses to individuality versus conformity generalizations.

Choice-Based Differentiated Products

Students may choose one of the following independent products to complete (*Note*: Use Rubric 1: Product Rubric in Appendix C to assess student products.):

- Apply a visual analysis to Escher's *Metamorphosis I-IV*. Compare it to *Day and Night* in an essay, addressing techniques, images, and main idea/message. Cite specific details from each piece of art in your analysis and relate your ideas to the major concept of conformity, individuality, or related concept about identity.
- Think of a song that matches the mood of the art *Day and Night*. Explain why the song complements the art with at least four supporting features of the music (lyrics, use of elements in music, etc.).
- Write a narrative or poem based on the setting displayed by *Day and Night*. Use descriptive language in your writing to develop the setting of your piece, and focus your story/poem on a major theme of the art.
- Draw a picture conveying the conflict of individuality versus conformity. Apply a feature of Escher's style to your work (such as use of symmetry or tessellations), and include a paragraph explaining the message of your work.

ELA Practice Tasks

Assign one of the following tasks as a performance-based assessment for this lesson:

- Write an essay in which you analyze in detail how a theme in one of Bradbury's short stories is revealed in Escher's art. In your analysis, be sure

	Concept/Theme
0	Provides no response.
1	Response is limited, vague, and/or inaccurate.
2	Response lacks adequate explanation. Response does not relate or create a generalization about individuality versus conformity.
3	Response is accurate and makes sense. Response relates to or creates an idea about individuality versus conformity with some relation to the art.
4	Response is accurate, insightful, and well written. Response relates to or creates a generalization about individuality versus conformity with evidence from the art.

Figure 3.2. Scoring guidelines for Lesson 3 formative assessment.

to compare how Bradbury and Escher's techniques develop this theme. Support your analysis with evidence from the text and art.

- How does our environment shape our identity? Use evidence from Escher's *Day and Night* and one of Bradbury's stories to support your answer. In an explanatory essay, address the question, explaining your response with evidence from both a story and the art.

Formative Assessment

1. Ask students to respond to the following prompt in a single paragraph: *What does* Day and Night *reveal about conformity versus individuality? Explain in a well-developed paragraph with support from the work. Be sure to relate to a conformity versus individuality generalization.*
2. Use the scoring guidelines in Figure 3.2 to evaluate students' assessments.

Name: _____ Date: _____

Handout 3.1
Blank Visual Analysis Wheel

Directions: Draw arrows across elements to show connections.

Art Piece: _____

Purpose/Context

Point of View

Images

Techniques

Emotions

Main Idea

Artist
Background

Structure/
Organization

Implications

Evaluation

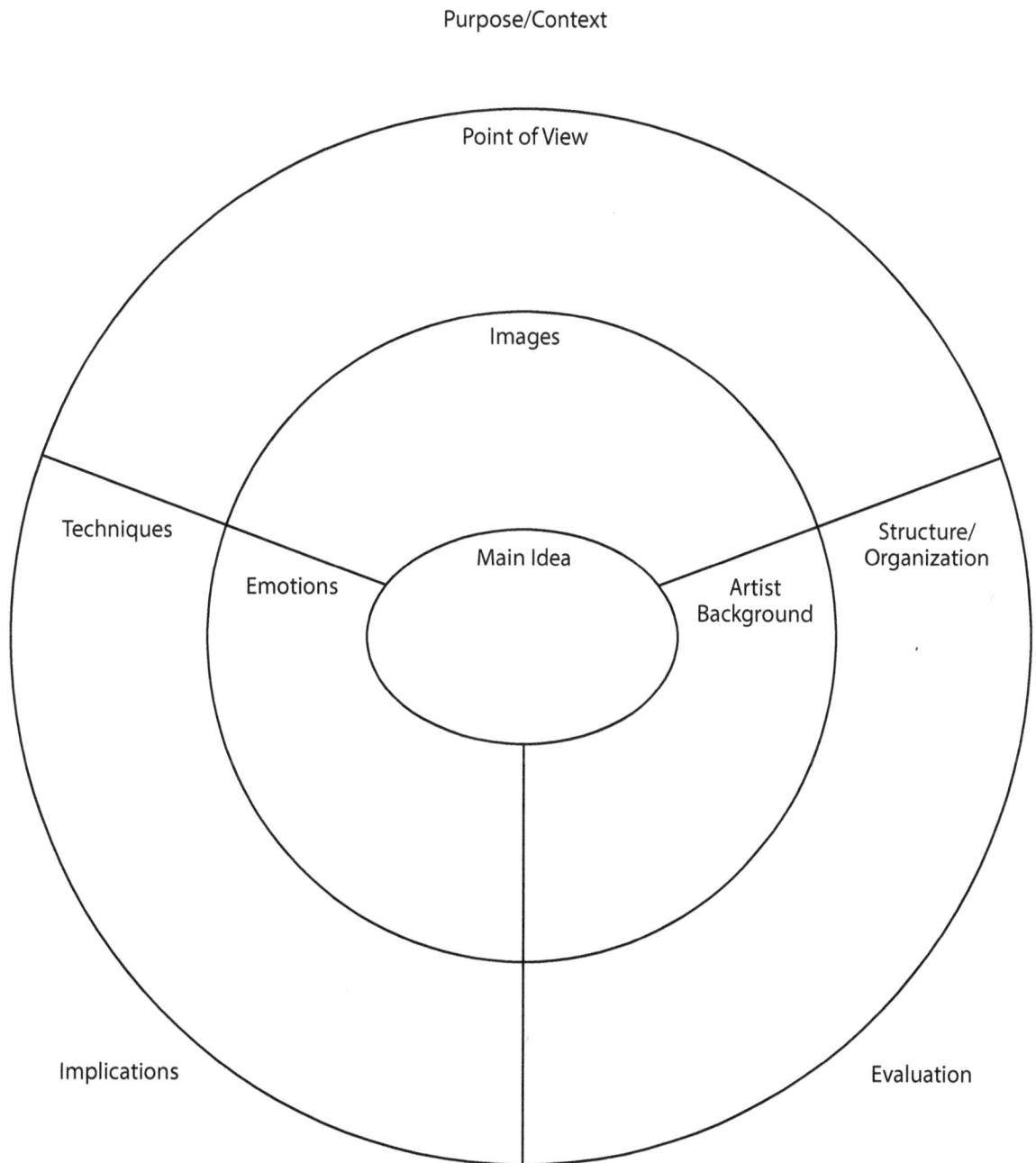

Created by Tamra Stambaugh, Ph.D., & Emily Mofield, Ed.D., 2015.

AN EXAMINATION
OF RISK
Against the Status Quo

DOI: 10.4324/9781003235620-8

Lesson

4

"Letter to DAR" and "My Day" Column
by Eleanor Roosevelt

Goals/Objectives

Content: To analyze and interpret texts and art, students will be able to:
- explain with evidence how a writer supports a claim,
- respond to interpretations of texts through a variety of contexts by justifying ideas and providing new information, and
- compare and contrast texts and real-world events on theme.

Process: To develop thinking, writing, and communication skills, students will be able to:
- reason through an issue by analyzing points of view, assumptions, and implications;
- use evidence to develop and support inferences;
- evaluate the use of effective argumentation; and
- analyze societal or individual conflicts resulting from the struggle between individuality versus conformity.

Concept: To understand the concept of individuality versus conformity in the language arts, students will be able to:
- support conformity versus individuality generalizations with evidence,
- develop and apply generalizations of additional key concepts, and
- explain the conflict between conformity and individuality.

Accelerated CCSS ELA Standards

RI.9-10.1	SL.9-10.1c
RI.9-10.2	SL.9-10.1d
RI.9-10.3	RH.9-10.1
RI.9-10.6	RH.9-10.2
RI.9-10.7	RH.9-10.8
RI.9-10.9	RH.9-10.9
SL.9-10.1	W.9-10.4

55

DOI: 10.4324/9781003235620-9

Materials

- Handout 1.3: Concept Organizer (continued from previous lessons)
- Handout 4.1: "Letter to DAR" by Eleanor Roosevelt and "Response From Mrs. Robert, President of DAR"
- Handout 4.2: "My Day" Newspaper Column by Eleanor Roosevelt
- Handout 4.3: Reasoning About a Situation or Event
- Rubric 1: Product Rubric (Appendix C)

Introductory Activity

Engage students in a quick debate. Ask: *Suppose you are a member of a group, and the group does something you do not approve. Should you work to persuade the group to change, or should you remove yourself from the group?* Students may stand on opposite sides of the room to debate their point of view.

Read Text

Instead of giving students a great deal of background information, tell students that they will be uncovering clues to a situation by looking at a few primary source documents. They will be reading correspondence between Eleanor Roosevelt and the Daughters of the American Revolution (DAR) society. Distribute Handout 4.1: "Letter to DAR" by Eleanor Roosevelt and "Response From Mrs. Robert, President of DAR." Allow students time to read both documents. Then lead them in a discussion. You may want to try a Socratic Seminar approach with a fishbowl discussion.

Text-Dependent Questions

These questions may be useful for a Socratic seminar or class discussion focused on Handout 4.1. Select from the following:

- What is the cause of the controversy?
- What do these documents reveal about Eleanor Roosevelt's character?
- What questions do you have about the context of these documents?
- What role does Eleanor Roosevelt's emotion play in the resignation letter? Consider her appeal to guilt and personal obligation.

Encourage students to ask questions to each other during this process. After discussion, explain to students that DAR banned Marian Anderson, an African-American singer, from singing at Constitution Hall in Washington, DC. Explain that later Marian Anderson was invited to sing at the Lincoln Memorial dedication in Washington, DC, bringing racial discrimination into the national spotlight. Ask students to consider the ironies of the controversy (i.e., Lincoln is being memorialized). This performance is available on YouTube.

Read Text

Explain that Eleanor Roosevelt wrote a syndicated newspaper column called "My Day." Distribute Handout 4.2: "My Day" Newspaper Column by Eleanor Roosevelt. Tell students: *In this excerpt, we have more insight into Eleanor Roosevelt's decision making. Read the column silently.*

Text-Dependent Questions

After reading Handout 4.2, select from the following questions for students to respond to in small groups:

- What additional insight do you have about Eleanor Roosevelt's decision making?
- What phrase in the document best supports her fight against the status quo?
- What does this document reveal about her character? Support this with textual evidence.
- What one word best describes Eleanor Roosevelt, based on this text? What evidence supports this?

In-Class Activity to Deepen Learning

Use Handout 4.3: Reasoning About a Situation or Event to reason through the issue "Should Eleanor Roosevelt resign from the DAR?" Help students realize that this decision may seem small, but it made a large statement to the nation about racial discrimination. As a First Lady, she also risked her husband's reputation. Figure 4.1 provides some sample responses.

- **Situation:** Should Eleanor Roosevelt resign from the DAR?
- **Stakeholders:** Eleanor Roosevelt, Marian Anderson, DAR Representatives, FDR.
- **Point of View:** How the stakeholder(s) would answer the question, including evidence of why they feel this way.
- **Assumptions:** The values and beliefs taken for granted by the stakeholders.
- **Implications:** The short- and long-term consequences that happened or could have happened if that particular point of view were actualized.

Stakeholders	Eleanor Roosevelt	Marian Anderson	DAR Representatives	Her Husband (President FDR)
Point of View	Yes; she should take a stand against racial discrimination—go against the group.	Yes; appreciates support and opportunity for equal treatment.	No; she should stay loyal to our cause and group.	Yes; supportive of wife, though it could risk what others think of him as president.
Assumptions	Assumes she can do no good remaining a member of the organization—she will not work to change their minds.	An important figure (Eleanor Roosevelt) cares about her work and equal opportunity.	Assumes that an African American should not sing to an integrated audience (assumes superiority).	Assumes the values of his wife.
Implications	Her stance developed a lasting awareness about civil rights and racial prejudice.	She was invited to sing at Lincoln Memorial—spotlight on her as an African American artist and racial prejudice.	After this incident, DAR realized the need to change. Today, the DAR honors her memory.	Lasting awareness about civil rights issues and racial prejudice.

Figure 4.1. *Should Eleanor Roosevelt resign from the DAR?* Sample responses.

Concept Connections

Lead students through a discussion using Handout 1.3: Concept Organizer, continued from previous lessons. Students should list examples about how the work demonstrates some of the generalizations. Figure 4.2 provides some sample responses.

Choice-Based Differentiated Products

Students may choose one of the following independent products to complete (*Note*: Use Rubric 1: Product Rubric in Appendix C to assess student products):

Both conformity and individuality are agents of change.
Eleanor Roosevelt's stance as an individual brought civil rights issues to the public eye.
Both conformity and individuality involve sacrifice.
Eleanor sacrificed her prestige as a member of the DAR and risked her and her husband's reputation.
There are positives and negatives to both conformity and individuality.
Eleanor Roosevelt gave up her status as a member of DAR, but helped set the stage that allowed others to have status as equal citizens in America.
Examine the relationship between conformity, individuality, and another related concept.
Challenging the status quo promotes societal change.

Figure 4.2. Sample student responses to individuality versus conformity generalizations.

- Read three additional "My Day" columns written by Eleanor Roosevelt. Create a product (PowerPoint, video documentary, brochure, pamphlet, monologue) that shows how Eleanor Roosevelt's individuality fought against the status quo during her time period. Also explain how her decision-making had long-term implications to today. Cite textual evidence from all three sources in your product.

- Study the style of Eleanor Roosevelt's "My Day" columns. Develop your own "My Day" column that addresses contemporary national issues using the same style Eleanor Roosevelt used. Be sure to include an idea relating to an individual questioning the status quo.

- Find various quotes of Eleanor Roosevelt that reflect her passion to promote positive change in society. Develop a collage with quotes, images, pictures, and symbols that represent Eleanor Roosevelt as a nonconformist who promoted change in society. Include at least 10 quotes from her texts, letters, or speeches.

ELA Practice Tasks

Assign one of the following tasks as a performance-based assessment for this lesson:

- Read three "My Day" columns (suggested source: http://www.gwu.edu/~erpapers/myday/browsebyyear.cfm) and explain the extent to which Eleanor Roosevelt was a nonconformist who promoted change during her lifetime. Use sufficient evidence from the texts to develop your reasoning in an explanatory essay and support your central idea.

	Inference From Evidence
0	Provides no response.
1	Response is limited, vague, and/or inaccurate. There is no justification for answers given.
2	Response is accurate, but lacks adequate explanation. Response includes some justification about the societal conflict.
3	Response is accurate and makes sense. Response includes some justification about the societal conflict.
4	Response is accurate, insightful, interpretive, and well written. Response includes thoughtful justification about the societal conflict.

Figure 4.3. Scoring guidelines for Lesson 4 formative assessment.

- Research more about the controversy around Marian Anderson singing at the Lincoln Memorial Dedication. Explain the causes of the controversy and explain the short- and long-term implications (effects). Use sufficient evidence from primary and secondary sources and cite your sources appropriately.

Formative Assessment

1. Ask students to respond to the following prompt in a single paragraph: *What can you infer is meant by the phrase "you had an opportunity to lead in an enlightened way" and how does it relate to the societal conflict?*
2. Use the scoring guidelines in Figure 4.3 to evaluate students' assessments.

Handout 4.1

"Letter to DAR" *by Eleanor Roosevelt*
and "Response From Mrs. Robert, President of DAR"

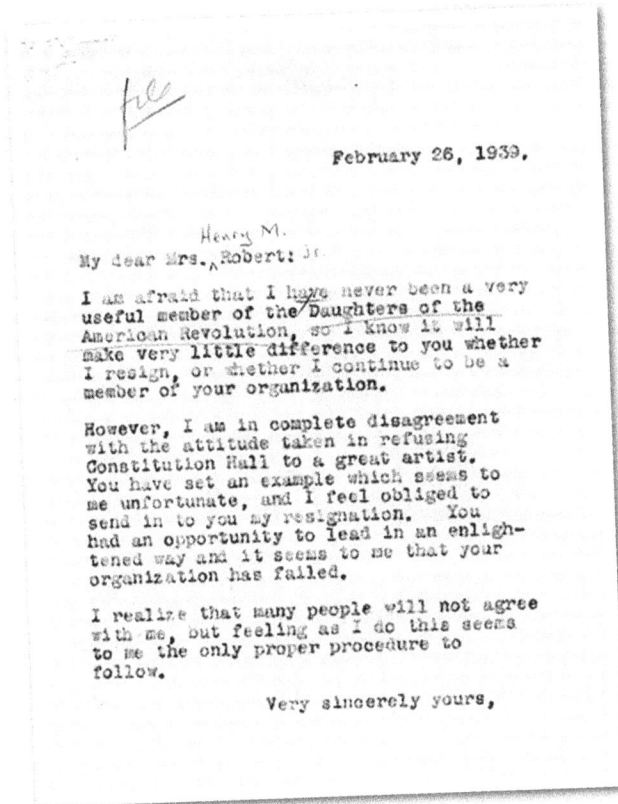

"Letter to DAR" by Eleanor Roosevelt
February 26, 1939

My dear Mrs. Henry M. Robert Jr.:

I am afraid that I have never been a very useful member of the Daughters of the American Revolution, so I know it will make very little difference to you whether I resign, or whether I continue to be a member of your organization.

However, I am in complete disagreement with the attitude taken in refusing Constitution Hall to a great artist. You have set an example which seems to me unfortunate, and I feel obliged to send in to you my resignation. You had an opportunity to lead in an enlightened way and it seems to me that your organization has failed.

I realize that many people will not agree with me, but feeling as I do this seems to me the only proper procedure to follow.

Very sincerely yours,

"Response From Mrs. Robert, President of DAR"

My dear Mrs. Roosevelt:

Your letter of resignation reaches me in Colorado upon my return from the far West. I greatly regret that you found this action necessary. Our society is engaged in the education for citizenship and the humanitarian service in which we know you to be vitally interested.

I am indeed sorry not to have been in Washington at this time. Perhaps I might have been able to remove some of the misunderstanding and to have presented to you personally the attitude of the society.

With best wishes always.

Very sincerely,

Name: _____   Date: _____

Handout 4.2
"My Day" Newspaper Column *by Eleanor Roosevelt*

February 27, 1939

Washington, Sunday—Here we are back in Washington. I woke this morning to what sounded like a real spring rain. The grass outside my window looks green and, though I suppose we will probably have a blizzard next week, at the moment I feel as though spring had really arrived.

I am having a very peaceful day. I drove my car a short distance out of the city this morning to pilot some friends of mine who are staring [starting] off for a vacation in Florida. I think this will be my only excurison [excursion] out of the White House today, for I have plenty of work to do on an accumulation of mail and I hope to get through in time to enjoy an evening of uninterrupted reading.

I have been debating in my mind for some time, a question which I have had to debate with myself once or twice before in my life. Usually I have decided differently from the way in which I am deciding now. The question is, if you belong to an organization and disapprove of an action which is typical of a policy, should you resign or is it better to work for a changed point of view within the organization? In the past, when I was able to work actively in any organization to which I belonged, I have usually stayed in until I had at least made a fight and had been defeated.

Even then, I have, as a rule, accepted my defeat and decided I was wrong or, perhaps, a little too far ahead of the thinking of the majority at that time. I have often found that the thing in which I was interested was done some years later. But, in this case, I belong to an organization in which I can do no active work. They have taken an action which has been widely talked of in the press. To remain as a member implies approval of that action, and therefore I am resigning.

I have just seen some people who are arranging for the Coronado Cuarto Centennial Celebration in New Mexico in 1940. All the plans for this celebration, which will begin in May 1940, sound interesting and delightful. New Mexico has many historic spots. There is beauty and an almost foreign interest in this state which has so many ties with Spain and the South and Central American countries. I hope that 1940 will see a great awakening of interest in this part of our nation. More of our American citizens than ever before should see this land of sunshine and color. I, for one, will make every effort to make the rounds of all the exhibitions which will be available during the summer following the opening of this celebration.

While we are speaking on interesting things in the West, let me tell you that I have been sent a pamphlet by the "Save the Redwoods League" of Berkeley, Calif., which pictures commercial exploitation of these beautiful redwood trees in the State of California. Anyone who has ever taken the drive up from the Yosemite to the State of Oregon, cannot fail to have an unforgettable picture of these giants of the forest. They have stood thousands of years. Perhaps some of them have reached maturity, but it seems to me a wicked thing to cut them down when that time arrives. Can not either the State or the Nation take a hand in preserving these forests?

—E. R.

Name: _____ Date: _____

Handout 4.3
Reasoning About a Situation or Event

What Is the Situation?

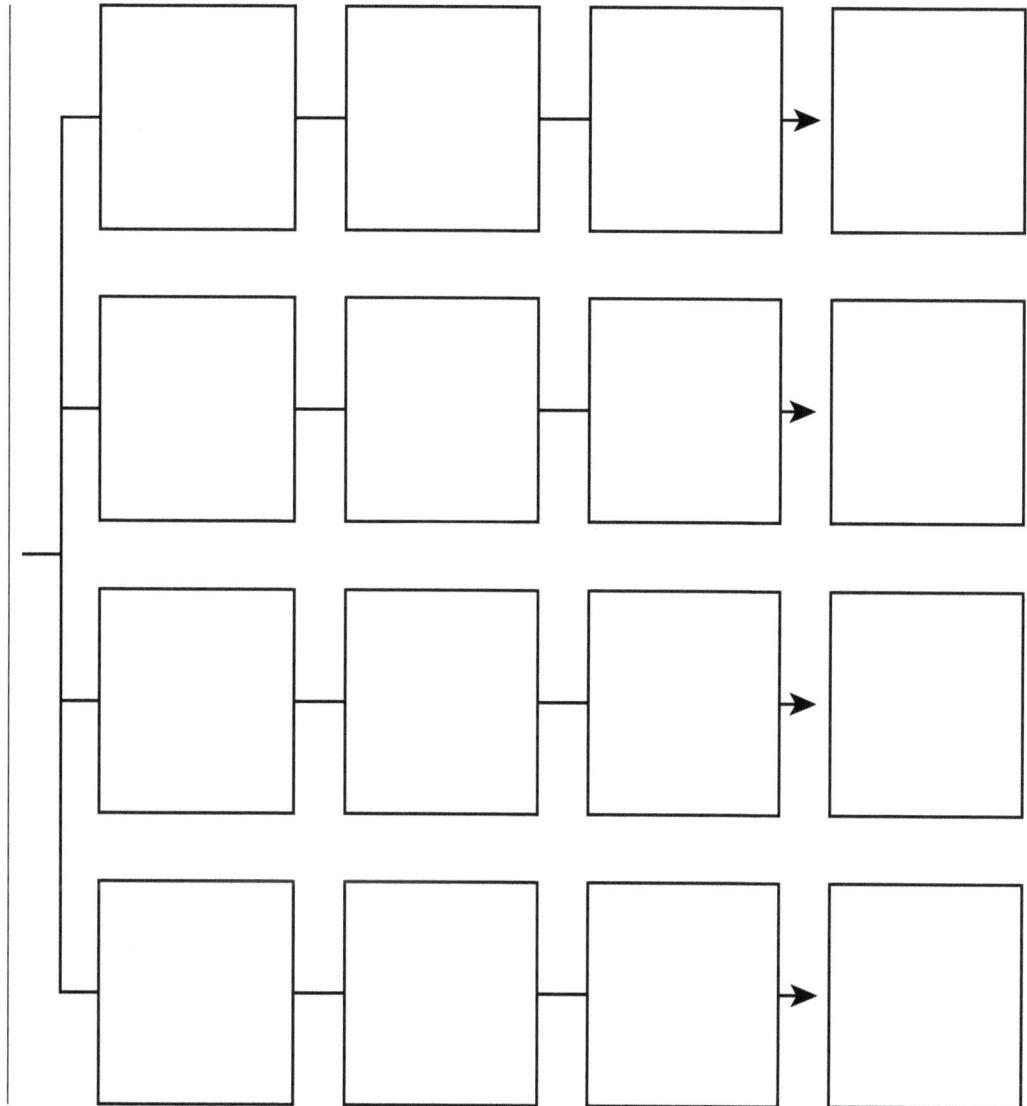

Stakeholders **Point of View** **Assumptions** **Implications**

Adapted from "Reasoning About a Situation or Event" by Center for Gifted Education, n.d., retrieved from http://education.wm.edu/centers/cfge/curriculum/teachingmodels. Copyright 2015 by William & Mary, Center for Gifted Education.

63

I, Me, You, We © Taylor & Francis

Lesson

5

Picasso's Guitars and Plato's Theory of Forms

Goals/Objectives

Content: To analyze and interpret texts and art, students will be able to:
- explain with evidence how literary and/or visual elements contribute to the overall meaning of a work,
- respond to interpretations of texts through a variety of contexts by justifying ideas and providing new information, and
- compare and contrast texts and real-world events on theme.

Process: To develop thinking, writing, and communication skills, students will be able to:
- use evidence to develop and support inferences, and
- analyze societal or individual conflicts resulting from the struggle between individuality versus conformity.

Concept: To understand the concept of individuality versus conformity in the language arts, students will be able to:
- support conformity versus individuality generalizations with evidence,
- develop and apply generalizations of additional key concepts, and
- explain the conflict between conformity and individuality.

Accelerated ELA CCSS Standards

RI.9-10.1	SL.9-10.1	W.9-10.4
RI.9-10.3	SL.9-10.1c	RI.9-10.7
SL.8.2	SL.9-10.1d	

Materials

- Pablo Picasso's *Still Life With Guitar, Variant State* (1913) to display, available at http://www.moma.org/visit/calendar/exhibitions/1101

DOI: 10.4324/9781003235620-10

- Various works by Picasso (available online)
- Handout 1.3: Concept Organizer (continued from previous lessons)
- Handout 5.1: Blank Visual Analysis Wheel
- Handout 5.2: Excerpts From Plato and Picasso
- Rubric 1: Product Rubric (Appendix C)

Introductory Activity

Ask students to draw a guitar. Have students share their drawings. Ask: *How would we evaluate who has the best drawing? How would we evaluate the best piece of art? Does it have to accurately reflect a real guitar?*

View Art

1. Show students the sculpture, *Still Life With Guitar, Variant State* (1913) (note that Picasso has several pieces of art featuring guitars, but this piece is a sculpture). Explain: *This piece is worth millions of dollars, and the student sketches are not. Why?* At the end of the lesson, students should have a better understanding of why.

2. Ask: *What comes to mind when I ask you to envision a sculpture? What's different about this guitar sculpture?* Students may refer to classical sculptures; during this time most sculptures were of people or things in nature—never before had anyone made a sculpture of a guitar because people already made guitars. Why would anyone make a sculpture of something already made by humans? Making a man-made guitar that's not really a guitar was a revolutionary idea.

3. Show other pieces by Picasso. Ask students to give titles to the works as you share them. Ask: *Is this artwork good? Who determines whether a piece of artwork is good: the majority or the individual?* Suggested pieces:
   - *Three Musicians*, 1921
   - *Guernica*, 1937
   - *The Old Guitarist*, 1903
   - *Child With a Dove*, 1901
   - *Woman in Hat and Fur Collar*, 1937
   - *Self Portrait*, 1907
   - *Don Quixote*, 1955
   - *Ma Jolie (My Pretty Girl)*, 1912
   - *Le pigeon aux petit pois (The Pigeon With Green Peas)*, 1911
   - *The Picasso in Chicago* (Public sculpture)

4. After showing students several of Picasso's works, ask students to describe Picasso's style. Ask: *How do you think photography may have influenced abstract art?* (Photograph as a new technology depicts real reality, so artists have freedom to move away from depicting exact reality.)

5. Give some background about Picasso (or ask students to do some initial research): *Pablo Picasso (1881–1973) is a Spanish artist who lived much of his adult life in France. He has hundreds of paintings, drawing, and sculptures. He is known for cofounding the Cubist movement in abstract art and collage making. In Cubism, Picasso would draw a picture, take apart an object's shape, and rearrange the pieces in an abstract form. When one looks at this art, the subject can be seen from several perspectives. In developing collage, Picasso would use newspaper, wallpaper, and other papers to produce a work of art. You will have an opportunity to look at samples and create your own collage later in the lesson.*

Visual Analysis

1. Tell students that they will be closely analyzing the first piece: *Still Life With Guitar, Variant State* (1913). This is one guitar of a series of guitar art produced by Picasso. You may want to consult Khan Academy's video, "The Language of Representation: Pablo Picasso's Guitar, 1912–1914" to prepare to guide students through the visual analysis, available at https://www.youtube.com/watch?v=bfy6IxsN_lg. Additional information can be found online at Artdaily: http://artdaily.com/news/44861/Picasso--Guitars-1912-1914-Examines-a-Moment-of-Radical-Experimentation-in-20th-Century-Art#.Ukt16YZQGSo.

2. Distribute Handout 5.1: Blank Visual Analysis Wheel and guide students in taking notes on the art form during class discussion. Sample questions and responses to lead analysis are provided. The suggested responses are derived from the aforementioned sources.

   - **Context/Purpose:**
     - *Provide context for students:* This art was produced in 1913 as a series of sculptures, 1912–1914.
     - *What do you think his purpose/motive is in creating this?* To question the essence of the depiction of reality and definition of art.

   - **Point of View/Assumptions:**
     - *What is his point of view toward representing reality? What are his assumptions?* He does not wish to depict a strict reality; yet he assumes that we all know it's a guitar from the features.

Images/Technique/Structure:

- **Images:** *How does Picasso achieve "guitar-ness" without actually making a guitar?* The contours on the side create the effect, yet they are not the same scale.
- **Technique:** *How do you think Picasso made this?* He actually drew the guitar on cardboard, then cut it out into eight pieces and assembled it. Students may enjoy watching this link: http://www.moma.org/explore/multimedia/videos/152. *What is significant about this technique?* It's a very different, creative way to create a sculpture.
- **Structure:** *How is this guitar different from a regular guitar?* What pops out of a regular guitar is actually popping in and vice versa; strings do not cross the sound hole.

Emotions/Technique/Structure:

- *What emotions does this evoke in you? How did the artist accomplish this?* Consider that some people have angry reactions to Picasso's abstract art because of the techniques he uses.

Artist Background/Technique/Structure:

- Review information provided in the lesson.

Main Idea:

- *What is Picasso's main idea and how do you know?* It makes us question the essence of a guitar; this is recognizable as a guitar, yet it's not a guitar.
- *What is Picasso conveying about the nature of reality in this art?* Many answers are acceptable; Picasso's work makes us question what is real. *What makes one version of a guitar better than another? What makes an object art? How is it possible that this looks like a guitar, but it is not at all a guitar?*

Implications:

- *What are the implications/consequences of viewing this art?* Many people were angry this was called art, but it challenged the definition of art and inspired abstract sculpture for the 20th century. This is one of the most influential works of the 20th century.

Evaluation:

- *Do you like this art? Would you hang it in your home? Was the artist successful in presenting his ideas? Justify your answers with evidence.*

Read Text

1. Distribute Handout 5.2: Excerpts From Plato and Picasso. Students should read Plato's excerpts for the purpose of finding connections with Picasso's art and Picasso's excerpt. After reading Excerpt 1, ask: *How does this excerpt relate to Picasso's* Guitar*?* Helpful hints: Plato's *Republic* explains his Theory of Forms, which relates to Picasso's ideas of "guitar-ness"; Picasso produced an imitation of a guitar, not a guitar itself. He is the "craftsman" able to imitate the "ideal" or "form" of guitar.

2. Then ask students to read Excerpts 2 and 3. Ask: *How does this relate to defining "good" art? How does Excerpt 2 relate to Excerpt 3?* Plato's *Phaedo* relates to the Picasso excerpt because Picasso's intention is to focus on the art itself, not the intention of art; just as Plato argues that beauty comes from beauty itself, not the intention of making the beauty from color or its shape.

3. You may wish to help students understand Plato's Theory of Forms by referring to the following description:

   > The Theory of Forms was first postulated by Plato. He argues that immaterial abstractions known as *Forms* (sometimes translated as *Ideas*) possess a more fundamental reality than the objects that we see and touch, which are actually imperfect, mimetic copies of the Forms. It is the Forms which are *true*, and the objects that we see are a dull kind of mirror, a *partial* reflection of the truth embodied in the Forms. A partial truth is not the whole truth, and it is in that sense that Picasso's lie can be understood. (Cromar, n.d., para. 7)

4. Ask students to focus specifically on "Picasso Speaks" and be prepared to discuss.

Text-Dependent Questions

These questions may be useful for a Socratic seminar or class discussion. Select from the following:

- What is Picasso's main concern in paragraph 1? (Sample response: He seems frustrated that people are applying research to the study of art.) How does this relate to Excerpt 2 from Plato? (Sample response: Beauty of a work is from beauty itself, not research behind its interpretation.)
- What does Picasso mean by "art is a lie that makes us realize truth"? (Sample response: Art isn't really reality, but it helps us think about what is reality.) How does this relate to Excerpt 1 from Plato?

- What does Picasso mean by "The artist must know the manner whereby to convince others of the truthfulness of his lies"? (Sample response: The artist must be aware of how he produces art.)
- How does Picasso address the contention that naturalism is in opposition to modern painting? (Sample response: He says that they cannot exist as the same thing.) How does this relate to his work *Still Life With Guitar*? (Sample response: The guitar is not natural in true form or in his art; it's man made. The natural is completely separate from the art.)
- What quote from this article can you relate to Picasso's *Still life With Guitar*? (Sample response: "Through art we express our conception of what nature is not." Picasso illustrates this in his guitar sculpture because it is a sculpture of something made by humans already; something that is entirely a conception of what nature is not.)
- How does the excerpt from Picasso reveal ideas related to individuality versus conformity? How does the excerpt show examples of *both* concepts? (Sample response: Conformity is revealed in the reference that Cubism is like all other forms of art; individuality is revealed in several instances in which Picasso addresses the status quo's assumptions of art).

In-Class Activities to Deepen Learning

Make connections. Ask: *How does this piece of art reflect ideas related to Escher's* Day and Night*? How does this piece of art reflect ideas related to other lessons?* (Sample response: It relates to Eleanor Roosevelt—part of a movement to inspire others.)

Concept Connections

Lead students through a discussion using Handout 1.3: Concept Organizer, continued from previous lessons. Students should list examples about how the work demonstrates some of these generalizations. Figure 5.1 provides some sample responses.

Choice-Based Differentiated Products

Students may choose one of the following independent products to complete (*Note*: Use Rubric 1: Product Rubric in Appendix C to assess student products):

- Experiment with Picasso's unique techniques by making your own sculpture out of cardboard or create your own collage out of newspaper prints, wallpaper, music sheets, or pieces of photographs. Start with an ordinary object. Draw it on paper, cardboard, or other materials. Cut it and reassem-

Both conformity and individuality are agents of change.
Picasso's unique style changed the way art is appreciated. Picasso challenges everyone's definition of guitar by making a guitar out of unique materials.
Both conformity and individuality involve sacrifice.
Picasso's art was first rejected, but is now widely acclaimed.
There are positives and negatives to both conformity and individuality.
Picasso's own style of "guitar" allows others to consider the definition of art; although some reject it as art.
Examine the relationship between conformity, individuality, and another related concept.
Students may examine relationship to freedom, status quo, power, or change.

Figure 5.1. Sample student responses to individuality versus conformity generalizations.

ble it in a creative way to reflect Picasso's style. Explain how your abstract art relates to "Picasso Speaks."

- Research more about Picasso's personal life. Find examples of how he battled individuality versus conformity. Give a presentation to the class showing at least five ways Picasso worked against the status quo. Include at least five images in your presentation.
- Compare and contrast Picasso's techniques between *Still Life With Guitar* (1913) and another Picasso piece (art, collage, or sculpture) using the Visual Analysis Wheel for each piece. Then note your interpretations and findings in a chart, Venn diagram, or short essay.

ELA Practice Tasks

Assign one of the following tasks as a performance-based assessment for this lesson:

- How did Picasso's notions of art influence future art movements? Write an article using evidence from "Picasso Speaks" and other relevant research to develop your response. Consult at least two additional sources in your research and cite sources appropriately in your article.
- Write an essay in which you explain how Plato's Theory of Forms can be used to interpret Picasso's art. Cite at least four quotes from Plato's *Republic* and/or *Phaedo* in your expository essay.
- Is Plato's *Still Life With Guitar* true art? In an argumentative essay, support your claim with evidence from the art form and textual evidence from other sources.

	Concept/Theme
0	Provides no response.
1	Response is limited, vague, and/or inaccurate.
2	Response lacks adequate explanation. Response does not relate or create a generalization about individuality versus conformity.
3	Response is accurate and makes sense. Response relates to or creates an idea about individuality versus conformity with some relation to the art.
4	Response is accurate, insightful, and well written. Response relates to or creates a generalization about individuality versus conformity with evidence from the art.

Figure 5.2. Scoring guidelines for Lesson 5 formative assessment.

Formative Assessment

1. Ask students to respond to the following prompt in a single paragraph: *What do Picasso's works reveal about the big idea of conformity versus individuality? Explain in a well-developed paragraph with support from the work. Be sure to relate to a conformity versus individuality generalization.*

2. Use the scoring guidelines in Figure 5.2 to evaluate students' assessments.

Name: _____ Date: _____

Handout 5.1
Blank Visual Analysis Wheel

Directions: Draw arrows across elements to show connections.

Art Piece: _____

Purpose/Context

Point of View

Images

Techniques

Emotions

Main Idea

Artist Background

Structure/ Organization

Implications

Evaluation

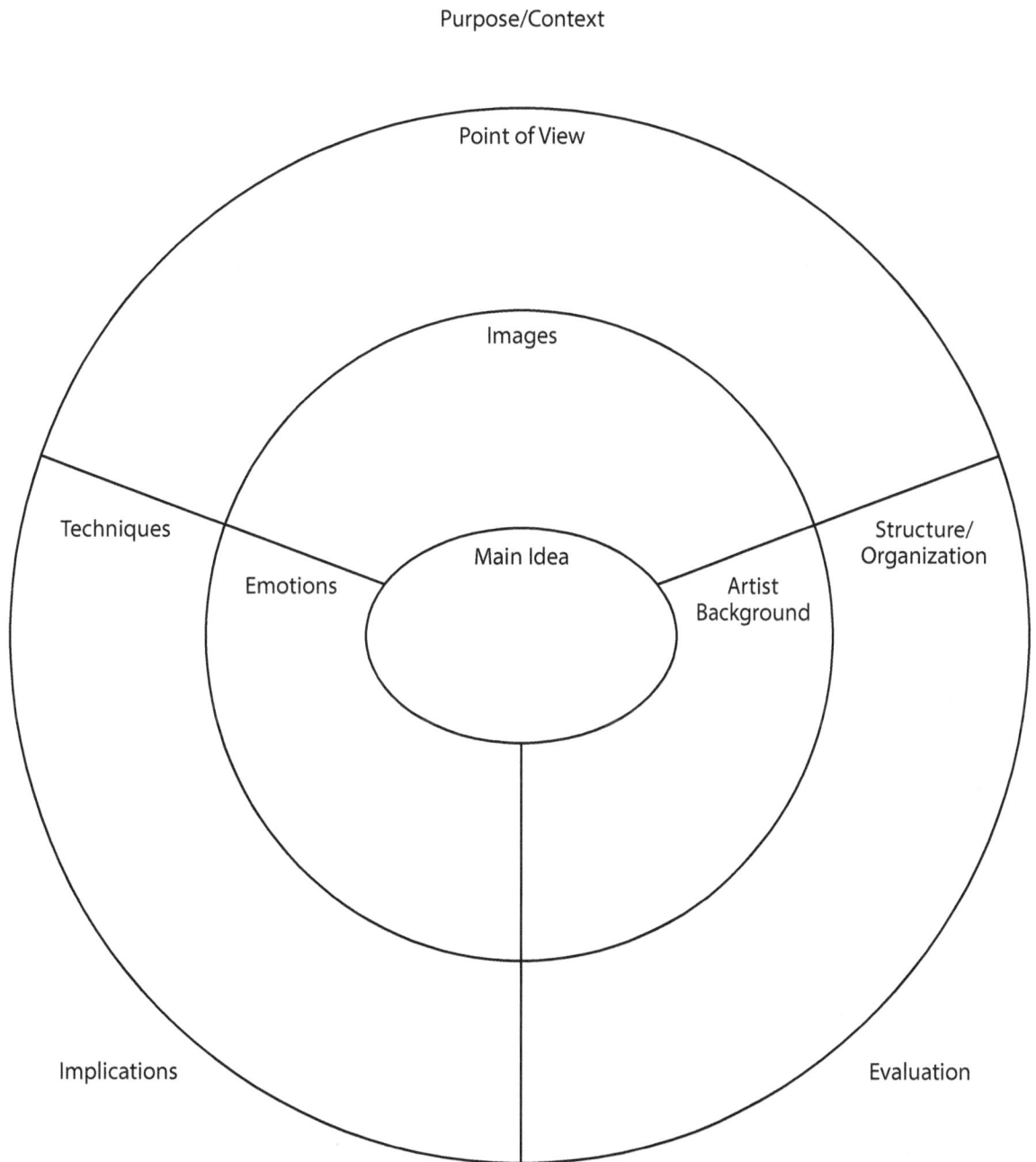

Created by Tamra Stambaugh, Ph.D., & Emily Mofield, Ed.D., 2015.

Handout 5.2
Excerpts From Plato and Picasso

Excerpt 1: From Plato's "Republic," 595c–596d

"Could you tell me in general what imitation is? For neither do I myself quite apprehend what it would be at." "It is likely, then," he said, "that I should apprehend!" "It would be nothing strange," said I, "since it often happens that the dimmer vision sees things in advance of the keener." "That is so," he said; "but in your presence I could not even be eager to try to state anything that appears to me, but do you yourself consider it." "Shall we, then, start the inquiry at this point by our customary procedure? We are in the habit, I take it, of positing a single idea or form in the case of the various multiplicities to which we give the same name. Do you not understand?" "I do." "In the present case, then, let us take any multiplicity you please; for example, there are many couches and tables." "Of course." "But these utensils imply, I suppose, only two ideas or forms, one of a couch and one of a table." "Yes." "And are we not also in the habit of saying that the craftsman who produces either of them fixes his eyes on the idea or form, and so makes in the one case the couches and in the other the tables that we use, and similarly of other things? For surely no craftsman makes the idea itself. How could he . . . ?"

Excerpt 2: From Plato's "Phaedo," 100:c–d

"Then," said he, "see if you agree with me in the next step. I think that if anything is beautiful besides absolute beauty it is beautiful for no other reason than because it partakes of absolute beauty; and this applies to everything. Do you assent to this view of cause?"

"I do," said he.

"Now I do not yet, understand," he went on, "nor can I perceive those other ingenious causes. If anyone tells me that what makes a thing beautiful is its lovely color, or its shape or anything else of the sort, I let all that go, for all those things confuse me, and I hold simply and plainly and perhaps foolishly to this, that nothing else makes it beautiful but the presence or communion (call it which you please) of absolute beauty, however it may have been gained; about the way in which it happens, I make no positive statement as yet, but I do insist that beautiful things are made beautiful by beauty. For I think this is the safest answer I can give to myself or to others, and if I cleave fast to this . . . "

Excerpt 3: From "Picasso Speaks," 1923

The following excerpted statement was made in Spanish to Marius de Zayas. Picasso approved de Zayas's manuscript before it was translated into English and published in *The Arts* (New York, May 1923) under the title "Picasso Speaks." In this excerpt, he speaks about his skepticism toward others trying to intellectualize Cubism.

Handout 5.2, Continued

I can hardly understand the given to the word *research* in connection with modern painting. In my opinion to search means nothing in painting. To find, is the thing. Nobody is interested in following a man who, with his eyes fixed on the ground, spends his life looking for the pocketbook that fortune should put in his path. The one who finds something no matter what it might be, even if his intention were not to search for it, at least arouses our curiosity, if not our admiration.

Among the several sins that I have been accused of committing, none is more false than the one that I have, as the principal objective in my work, the spirit of research. When I paint, my object is to show what I have found and not what I am looking for. In art intentions are not sufficient and, as we say in Spanish: love must be proved by facts and not by reasons. What one does is what counts and not what one had the intention of doing.

We all know that Art is not truth. Art is a lie that makes us realize truth, at least the truth that is given us to understand. The artist must know the manner whereby to convince others of the truthfulness of his lies. If he only shows in his work that he has searched, and re-searched, for the way to put over lies, he would never accomplish anything.

The idea of research has often made painting go astray, and made the artist lose himself in mental lucubrations*. Perhaps this has been the principal fault of modern art. The spirit of research has poisoned those who have not fully understood all the positive and conclusive elements in modern art and has made them attempt to paint the invisible, and therefore, the unpaintable.

They speak of naturalism in opposition to modern painting. I would like to know if anyone has ever seen a natural work of art. Nature and art, being two different things, cannot be the same thing. Through art we express our conception of what nature is not . . . .

Cubism is no different from any other school of painting. The same principles and the same elements are common to all. The fact that for a long time cubism has not been understood and that even today there are people who cannot see anything in it, means nothing. I do not read English, an English book is a blank book to me. This does not mean that the English language does not exist, and why should I blame anybody else but myself if I cannot understand what I know nothing about? . . .

*Lucubration: a piece of learned writing; a written work resulting from prolonged study, often having a scholarly or pedantic style.

Lesson

6

"Much Madness is divinest Sense"
by Emily Dickinson

Goals/Objectives

Content: To analyze and interpret texts and art, students will be able to:

- explain with evidence how literary and/or visual elements contribute to the overall meaning of a work,
- respond to interpretations of texts through a variety of contexts by justifying ideas and providing new information, and
- compare and contrast texts and real-world events on theme.

Process: To develop thinking, writing, and communication skills, students will be able to:

- use evidence to develop and support inferences, and
- analyze societal or individual conflicts resulting from the struggle between individuality versus conformity.

Concept: To understand the concept of individuality versus conformity in the language arts, students will be able to:

- support conformity versus individuality generalizations with evidence,
- develop and apply generalizations of additional key concepts, and
- explain the conflict between conformity and individuality.

Accelerated CCSS ELA Standards

RL.9-10.1	SL.9-10.1	SL.9-10.4
RL.9-10.2	SL.9-10.1c	W.9-10.4
RL.9-10.4	SL.9-10.1d	

Materials

- Video: "Asch Conformity Experiment," available at https://www.youtube.com/watch?v=TYIh4MkcfJA

 DOI: 10.4324/9781003235620-11

- Student copies of "Much Madness is divinest Sense" by Emily Dickinson, available at http://www.poetryfoundation.org/poem/182156
- Student copies of "I'm Nobody! Who are You?" by Emily Dickinson, available at http://www.poets.org/poetsorg/poem/im-nobody-who-are-you-260
- Handout 6.1: Prereading Activity
- Handout 6.2: Blank Literary Analysis Wheel
- Handout 6.3: Big Idea Reflection
- Rubric 1: Product Rubric (Appendix C)

Introductory Activities

1. Introduce the lesson by explaining or showing a video about Solomon Asch's famous conformity experiment. A participant is shown a card with three lines and is asked to identify the line that is of the same length as one on a card. The other participants have been told beforehand to give the incorrect answer, and usually the participant also gives the incorrect answer because everyone else did. At teacher discretion, consider doing a modified experiment as a simulation (suggested source available at http://www.simplypsychology.org/asch-conformity.html).

2. Ask: *Why did participants conform so quickly to the majority? What does this reveal about the nature of human nature?*

3. Distribute Handout 6.1: Prereading Activity. The words to the poem "Much Madness is divinest Sense" are written in alphabetical order. Short words such as *the*, *a*, and *is* are taken out. The capitalization is how it appears in the poem. Review words students need to know to gain meaning. A few examples are:
   - **Divinest:** Connected with, coming from God; pleasing, attractive, well-performed; connected with worship
   - **Discerning:** Showing good judgment
   - **Assent:** An expression of agreement or acceptance
   - **Sane:** Mentally healthy
   - **Demur:** To object mildly to what you do not want to do but have been asked to do

   As suggested on the handout, ask students to develop their own poem using these words (and other words). Allow students to share responses. Then, read aloud the original poem by Emily Dickinson.

Read Text

Distribute or display "Much Madness is divinest Sense" and "I'm Nobody! Who are You?" Focus the close reading on "Much Madness is divinest Sense."

Text-Dependent Questions

Select from the following text-dependent questions for leading a Socratic seminar or class discussion:

- Paraphrase the first two lines of "Much Madness is divinest Sense" in your own words. (Sample response: To someone who has good judgment, it's a good thing to be "mad.")
- What does "Madness" mean in this context? Is it about being angry or insane? How do you know?
- What is significant about Dickinson's word choice of "demur"? What does this connotation evoke as opposed to related words such as "protest"?
- What effect does the chiastic structure of Lines 1 and 3 have on the poem? (Sample response: She is developing contrast; chiastic structure is a reversal in word order like "Ask not what your country can do for you, but what you can do for your country." This can be marked so that similar words are connected with an X when written out on two lines.)
- Why is Dickinson developing this contrast in meaning with the word "Sense?" (Sample response: Sense is defined by what the majority thinks [Line 4] and sometimes what the majority thinks is sensible is actually crazy.)
- What is significant about the word "divinest" in the first line? (Sample response: This word is not capitalized, while the other words are. It's also in superlative. Of all words to be capitalized, since this one has a connotation about God, one would think that it should be capitalized. Perhaps she is going against the grain, as the poem's message implies, and not capitalizing the word that should probably be capitalized).
- How does "assent - and you are sane" relate to the theme of conformity versus individuality?
- Why is "Chain" capitalized? What meanings does this word imply in regard to a person's freedom? (Sample response: Disagreeing with majority involves to some extent a loss of freedom.)
- How does the use of the dash affect the meaning of the poem? (Sample response: The dash is used instead of a comma; an expert in grammar may argue that she overuses the dash, but perhaps she is doing this to illustrate the point of the poem—she is going against sensible rules in being a nonconformist poet. It also illustrates the speed of judgment the majority has on those who disagree with majority.)

According to the poem, who decides what is madness? (Sample response: The majority.) How does this relate to the meaning of the poem? (Sample response: Madness is determined by perspective.)

How does the chronology of the poem affect the theme of individuality versus conformity? (Sample response: The first two lines are positive, revealing independent freedom. The last two lines are negative, indicative of bondage. The middle lines show the progression from individuality to societal expectations.)

How do the last two lines shape Emily Dickinson's tone?

What new title would you give the poem? Defend your answer with ideas from the poem.

Literary Analysis

Note: You may wish to consult analyses online before guiding student discussion. Some ideas in this analysis are adapted from GradeSaver, available at http://www.gradesaver.com/emily-dickinsons-collected-poems/study-guide/summary-much-madness-is-divinest-sense-.

1. Guide students through a literary analysis using Handout 6.3: Blank Literary Analysis Wheel. Lead students through a basic discussion of each literary element, then emphasize the interaction of the elements with more complex questions. Encourage students to cite textual evidence throughout discussion. Students can take notes on the wheel and draw arrows to illustrate connections between concepts.

2. Focus on the following complex questions:

    How does the structure and punctuation of the poem contribute to the theme?

    How does Dickinson's tone enhance the theme?

    How does Dickinson's word choice contribute to the development of conflict in the poem?

3. The following notes may be helpful in guiding students through the analysis:

    Themes: Majority versus minority, oppression from being different, rebellion, individuality versus conformity, sanity versus insanity.

    Character: Consider only "you" is referred to throughout the poem. The poem clearly illustrates consequences for assenting and demurring. The use of "you" makes the poem more personal and applicable to reader.

    Setting: Because there is no setting, this allows the reader to consider that this poem can be applied to all people everywhere.

- **Conflicts:** Insanity versus sanity; individuality versus conformity; majority versus minority.
- **Structure:** The first two lines are positive, revealing independent freedom. The last two lines are negative, indicative of bondage. The middle lines show the progression from individuality to societal expectations.
- **Language:** Repetition of madness; significance of "Chain"; demur versus "rebel." Dickinson's attitude (tone) toward society is sneering, disdainful, and disapproving.
- **Symbols:** Discuss "Chain" (oppression of majority) and "Eye" (perspective—insane people are the ones who are actually sane).
- **Point of View:** Focus on how Dickinson wants us to consider how the majority shapes point of view. The majority defines sense and madness, making truth elusive.
- **Context:** Provide historical background knowledge on the poem. This was written by Dickinson who lived 1830–1886. The poem was first published in 1955. Dickinson lived in Amherst, MA. Her works were published posthumously. She has been considered insane both in her life and after her death. One may consider, was she really insane or a genius? What would be her motivation to write this poem? Students may wish to research more about her life background to answer these questions.

Big Idea Reflection

(Optional) Use Handout 6.3: Big Idea Reflection to connect the poem to real life. Students may work in small groups.

- **Concepts:** Freedom, oppression.
- **Generalizations:** What generalization about Conformity versus Individuality do you see as most evident in the poem? What other generalizations can be made?
- **Problem:** To be with majority or not; both individuality and conformity can lead to bondage.
- **Insight:** "Madness" is a matter of perspective.
- **World/Community/Individual:** Individual—Am I like everyone else so that others don't think I'm crazy? Am I the real me? Do I get put down for being my real self?
- **Solutions/Implications:** How might I respond to these issues in my life/world? What are the implications of these ideas on my life?

In-Class Activities to Deepen Learning

1. **Engage students in a quick debate.** Ask: *Is it better to be yourself and be shamed by the majority, or to give up part of yourself to be accepted by the majority?* Students can stand on opposite sides of the room to debate. Students may discuss their opinions.

2. Ask students to read "I'm Nobody! Who are You?" Ask them to apply the Blank Literary Analysis Wheel (Handout 6.2) and/or Big Idea Reflection (Handout 6.3) independently or in pairs. Discuss findings in a whole-class discussion.

3. Ask students to compare Dickinson's poems. Lead the class in a discussion by developing a comparison chart or Venn diagram. What are the conceptual similarities and how does the author use word choice to convey this? (Students could also compare "Much Madness is divinest Sense" to the pretest fable, "Parable of the Poison Well.")

4. Make connections. Ask: *How does "Much Madness is divinest Sense" relate to the Asch Conformity Experiment? Use specific lines in the poem to articulate connections.*

5. Have students create a piece of art that reflects the ideas in one of the poems studied in this lesson. Have students consider applying either Escher- or Picasso-like styles to their art and consider creating a symbolic instead of a literal depiction of the poem.

Concept Connections

Discuss connections to individuality versus conformity by asking the following questions. Students may reflect on concept connections using Handout 1.3: Concept Organizer, continued from previous lessons. Figure 6.1 provides some sample responses.

- How does reputation relate to a conformity generalization?
- What is the motivation to conform, according to the poem?

Choice-Based Differentiated Products

Students may choose one of the following independent products to complete (*Note*: Use Rubric 1: Product Rubric in Appendix C to assess student products):

- Learn more about Emily Dickinson's personal life. Write out interview questions and answers from her perspective. Include questions related to conformity versus individuality and her motivation behind writing the poems studied in this lesson. Perform the mock interview in a video (or live) in front of your classmates. Be ready to cite evidence for your responses.

Both conformity and individuality are agents of change.
People may change to conform to the majority to avoid being considered crazy, or to avoid being "handled with a Chain."
Both conformity and individuality involve sacrifice.
Being an individual involves a loss of reputation and/or freedom.
There are positives and negatives to both conformity and individuality.
To "demur" the majority with individuality may cause others to see the individual as crazy.
Examine the relationship between conformity, individuality, and another related concept.
Students may examine relationship to freedom, status quo, and oppression.

Figure 6.1. Sample student responses to individuality versus conformity generalizations.

- Think about how "Much Madness is divinest Sense" relates to another lesson in this unit. Develop your own short story or nonfiction narrative in which two ideas merge. For example, develop a narrative about Picasso referring to the poem, or a fictional story in which Mr. Bittering from "Dark They Were and Golden-Eyed" thinks about this poem in an internal conflict.
- Think of a song that relates to the big ideas in one of Dickinson's poems ("Much Madness is divinest Sense" or "I'm Nobody! Who are You?"). In a comparison chart, Venn diagram, or essay, provide textual evidence from both the song and poem of how they each show similar ideas. Quote at least three phrases from the poem and three phrases from the song.
- Watch the world news and make a connection with the theme of majority versus minority in "Much Madness is divinest Sense." Explain the connection in a reflection. Also answer the following questions: What is the societal problem and what solutions are offered? What new solutions can you think of that could also address the problem?

ELA Practice Tasks

Assign one of the following tasks as a performance-based assessment for this lesson:

- In a well-developed essay, describe how Dickinson's use of structure, punctuation, and capitalization contribute to the main message of the poem. Cite relevant and sufficient evidence from the poem to develop your response.
- In a well-developed essay, describe how Emily Dickinson develops similar themes in "I'm Nobody! Who are You?" and "Much Madness is divinest

	Inference From Evidence
0	Provides no response.
1	Response is limited, vague, and/or inaccurate. There is no justification for answers given.
2	Response is accurate, but lacks adequate explanation. Response includes some justification about the conflict.
3	Response is accurate and makes sense. Response includes some justification about the conflict.
4	Response is accurate, insightful, interpretive, and well written. Response includes thoughtful justification about the conflict.

Figure 6.2. Scoring guidelines for Lesson 6 formative assessment.

Sense." Refer to specific literary techniques while citing textual evidence in your response.

- Which character or person from previous unit lessons is most like the speaker in the poem "Much Madness is divinest Sense?" Consider Mr. Bittering, Margot, Eleanor Roosevelt, and Picasso. Write an essay in which you develop your argument, citing evidence from the poem and a previous text in this unit to support your claim.

Formative Assessment

1. Ask students to respond to the following prompt in a single paragraph: *What is meant by "Assent - and you are sane - / Demur - you're straightway dangerous?" How does it relate to the main conflict in the poem?*
2. Use the scoring guidelines in Figure 6.2 to evaluate students' assessments.

Handout 6.1
Prereading Activity

all assent Chain
dangerous demur discerning
divinest Eye
handled Madness Madness Majority much much prevail sane Sense Sense
starkest straightway

1. Just by looking at these words, what do you think the poem is about?

2. What words do you need to know?

3. Using some of the words above and a few basic words (e.g., *the*, *is*, *are*, *it's*), create your own poem.

Handout 6.2
Blank Literary Analysis Wheel

Directions: Draw arrows across elements to show connections.

Text: _____

Purpose/Context

Setting

Mood

Language
Structure
Style

Symbols

Plot/
Conflict

Characters

Theme

Point of View

Tone

Interpretation

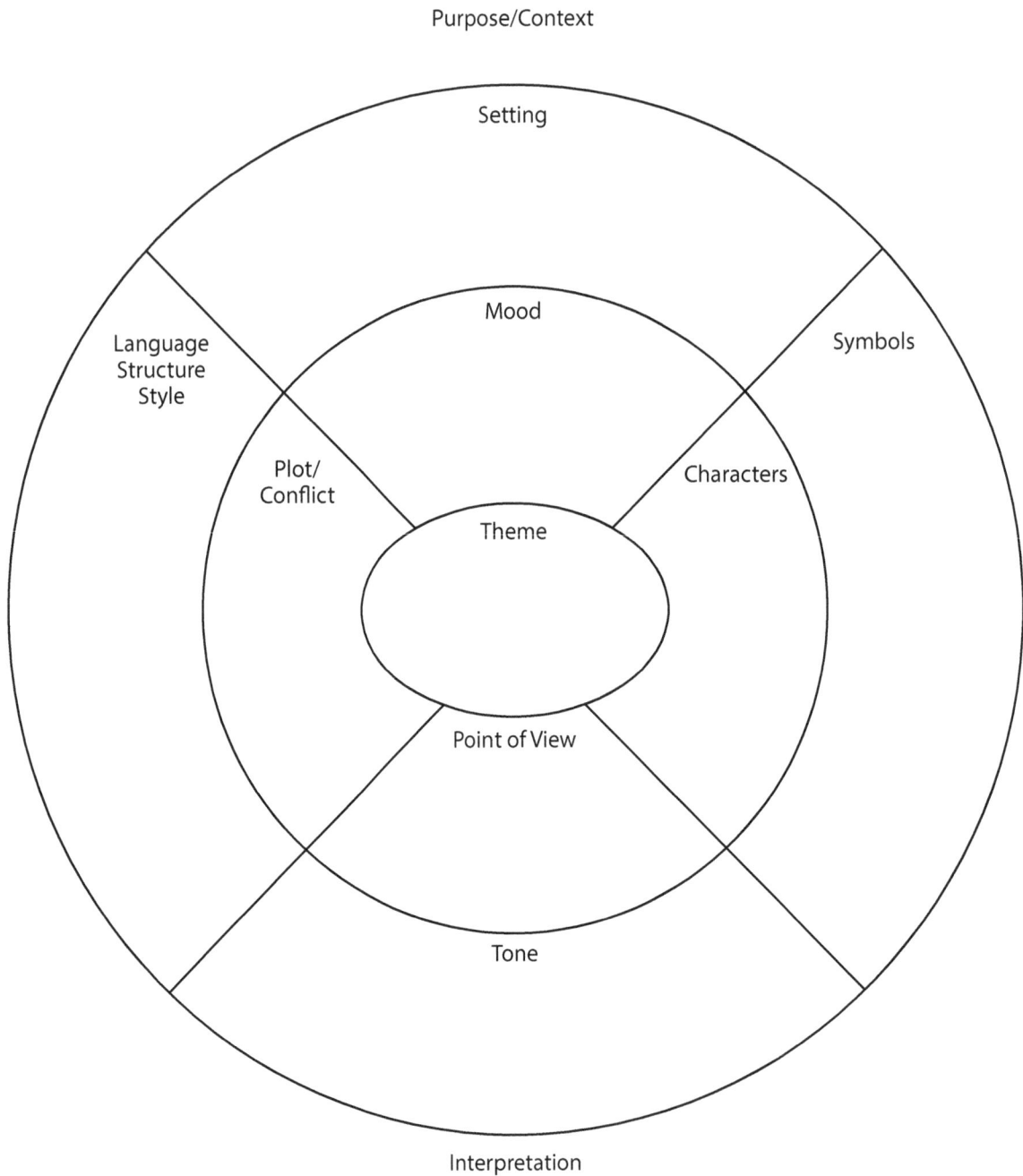

Created by Tamra Stambaugh, Ph.D., & Emily Mofield, Ed.D., 2015.

Name: _____ Date: _____

Handout 6.3
Big Idea Reflection

<table>
<tr>
<td rowspan="3">What?</td>
<td>Concepts:
What concepts/ideas are in the text?</td>
<td></td>
</tr>
<tr>
<td>Generalizations:
What broad statement can you make about one or more of these concepts? Make it generalizable beyond the text.</td>
<td></td>
</tr>
<tr>
<td>Issue:
What is the main issue, problem, or conflict?</td>
<td></td>
</tr>
<tr>
<td rowspan="2">So What?</td>
<td>Insight:
What insight on life is provided from this text?</td>
<td></td>
</tr>
<tr>
<td>World/Community/Individual:
How does this text relate to you, your community, or your world? What question does the author want you to ask yourself?</td>
<td></td>
</tr>
<tr>
<td>Now What?</td>
<td>Implications:
How should you respond to the ideas in the text? What action should you take? What are the implications of the text? What can you do with this information?</td>
<td></td>
</tr>
</table>

Created by Emily Mofield, Ed.D., & Tamra Stambaugh, Ph.D., 2015.

I, Me, You, We © Taylor & Francis

AN EXAMINATION OF SOCIAL CONFORMITY

DOI: 10.4324/9781003235620-12

Lesson

7

The Mayflower Compact
by William Bradford

Goals/Objectives

Content: To analyze and interpret texts and art, students will be able to:
- explain with evidence how a writer supports a claim,
- respond to interpretations of texts through a variety of contexts by justifying ideas and providing new information,
- compare and contrast texts and real-world events on theme, and
- evaluate rhetoric within primary sources.

Process: To develop thinking, writing, and communication skills, students will be able to:
- reason through an issue by analyzing points of view, assumptions, and implications;
- use evidence to develop and support inferences;
- evaluate the use of effective argumentation; and
- analyze societal or individual conflicts resulting from the struggle between individuality versus conformity.

Concept: To understand the concept of individuality versus conformity in the language arts, students will be able to:
- support conformity versus individuality generalizations with evidence,
- develop and apply generalizations of additional key concepts, and
- explain the conflict between conformity and individuality.

Accelerated CCSS ELA Standards

RI.9-10.1	RI.9-10.9	RH.9-10.2
RI.9-10.2	SL.9-10.1	RH.9-10.5
RI.9-10.3	SL.9-10.1c	RH.9-10.8
RI.9-10.5	SL.9-10.1d	RH.9-10.9
RI.9-10.6	RH.9-10.1	W.9-10.4

 DOI: 10.4324/9781003235620-13

Materials

- Handout 1.3: Concept Organizer
- Handout 7.1: The Mayflower Compact
- Handout 7.2: Blank Rhetorical Analysis Wheel
- Handout 7.3: Reasoning About a Situation or Event
- Rubric 1: Product Rubric (Appendix C)

Introductory Activities

1. Introduce three essential questions regarding the individual as part of society. Students may discuss these questions (VanTassel-Baska, 1988, pp. 274–275) with partners, whole group, or in quick writes:
   - Is it natural for an individual to want to contribute to his society?
   - What must humans do to ensure the survival of their society?
   - What conflicts does an individual face as a member of society?

2. Introduce the lesson by asking students to guess information about the *Mayflower* voyage.
   - How many passengers do you think were on the *Mayflower*? 102.
   - How many passengers do you think were males? 74. Females? 28.
   - How many passengers do you think were actual Separatists (later known as pilgrims)? 37. Many others were merchants, crewmembers, and others recruited to plant settlements in the "New World."

3. Provide additional background information: *The Mayflower left England in September 1620 and arrived at Cape Cod in November. The Separatists (pilgrims) fled the hostile political environment in England to the more peaceful Holland. However, while in Holland they were concerned about losing their cultural identity, so they decided to establish a new English colony. The passengers experienced great hardship and were delayed due to structural damage on the ship, which caused tension among crewmembers and passengers. They were supposed to arrive at the Colony of Virginia, but strong seas forced them to go back to Cape Cod. Here, they established The Mayflower Compact and signed it on the* Mayflower *in November 1620. A few set out on a search expedition for settlement, but encountered the harsh winter climate of the area. In December, they relocated to Plymouth and settled, but 45 of the 102 passengers died that winter of disease, from lack of shelter, or from general conditions on board ship.*

4. Divide students into small groups. Tell students: *Discuss the following scenario: Imagine coming to the "New World" from Holland in 1620. Brainstorm*

a list of problems you would encounter. After groups discuss, put all groups' ideas on the board. Ask students to then categorize these problems in groups. Discuss the categorization; ask students to prioritize the problems to address. Explain that students will read a document and infer the priorities of these individuals. Ask: *Why might it be important to cooperate with the group based on this scenario? Are there scenarios when individuality might be more important?*

Read Text

Distribute Handout 7.1: The Mayflower Compact. Ask students to read it once silently, then ask a student to read it aloud.

Text-Dependent Questions

Select from the following text-dependent questions to lead class discussion:
- Round robin: What word is most important in the text? (Everyone go around and answer.) Why did you choose this word?
- In small groups, ask students to create 3–4 word association webs. Students will categorize similar words in a web (e.g., all words related to "mutual," all words related to "religion," all words related to "authority/government," all words related to "promise"). Do not assign categories. Help students discover their own categories as they recognize patterns in the language.
- According to the text, to whom are the signers loyal?
- What is meant by the word "dread"? (*Note:* It means awe-inspiring, inspiring fear.)
- According to the text to whom are they making a promise? Why are they making this promise? What evidence supports this?
- What is significant about the word "covenant" to the overall meaning of the documents?
- Which phrase describes the primary purpose of this document?
- What is meant by "Civil Body Politic"?
- What can we infer is a priority for these signers?
- Additional questions to promote thinking (optional):
  • Why might some passengers not sign the document?
  • In what ways must the signers of The Mayflower Compact conform? What are they conforming to? Must they be required to give up some parts of their individual interests?
  • Would this be a positive or negative experience?
  • What might happen if the passengers did not sign?

- In what ways does the text show the signers are acting as *nonconformists*? (Sample response: They are planting a new English colony as Separatists . . . something never done before. This was the second permanent English colony, second to Jamestown).

Reveal to students that only 41 signed the document (but keep in mind that women were represented by their husbands).

Rhetorical Analysis

1. Briefly explain Aristotle's Elements of Rhetoric. Aristotle's rhetoric includes logos, ethos, and pathos appeals. This enhances a writer's ability to communicate with an audience (usually for persuasion).

    Logos: How the author establishes good reasoning to make the document/speech make sense. This includes major points, use of evidence, syllogisms, examples, evidence, facts, statistics, etc. Text-focused.

    Pathos: How the author appeals to the audience's emotion. Audience-focused.

    Ethos: How the author develops credibility and trust. Author-focused.

2. Using Handout 7.2: Blank Rhetorical Analysis Wheel, guide students through understanding the main claim in The Mayflower Compact. Students will examine how the writer achieves his purpose by analyzing how several factors work together to create an effective argument. This includes thinking about the rhetorical situation (e.g., purpose, context, audience), means of persuasion (ethos, logos, and pathos appeals), and rhetorical strategies (e.g., techniques, evidence, organization, etc.). Emphasize specific elements first (e.g. logos, pathos, ethos, organization, techniques, and point of view), then move toward combining elements for more complexity (e.g., what techniques does he use to develop pathos appeals; where are they placed and why?). Note the inner wheel conceptually spins so that its elements interact with each other and the outer wheel. Refer to Appendix A for detailed instructions about the Rhetorical Analysis Wheel and how to make a hands-on model.

3. The Rhetorical Analysis Wheel Guide (Appendix B) shows specific prompts to guide students in thinking through each separate concept. They may take notes on the Blank Rhetorical Analysis Wheel using arrows to show how concepts relate. It is suggested that students first note the answers to each concept separately on the graphic organizer, and then discuss how they relate. Consider making a poster of the Rhetorical Analysis Wheel Guide to refer to throughout the unit. *Note:* For a simpler version of this model, see Appendices A and B. This text analysis does not focus on the rhetorical

appeals (logos, ethos, and pathos) to support a claim; rather it focuses on why the author chose to use specific points to advance a central idea. Sample questions to lead the rhetorical analysis include:

- **Context/Purpose:**
  - *What is the historical context?* November 11, 1620. It is an agreement for passengers.
  - *What is Bradford's purpose?* To make a covenant promise to each other to govern themselves for their own survival.

- **Claim:**
  - *What is the main claim?* The passengers combine themselves to govern themselves.

- **Point of View/Assumptions:**
  - *What is the point of view of the author? What assumptions are made?* Bradford has a positive view toward cooperating as a self-governed civil body. Loyalty to King James is assumed.

- **Logos:**
  - *What are the main points?* They came to plant a colony and will govern themselves.
  - *How is this rationale developed?* Bradford appeals to the purpose for coming to the colony and states the reason for the compact ("for better ordering and preservation").

- **Pathos/Techniques/Structure:**
  - *What are the emotional appeals and how were they developed through specific techniques? Where are they in the document and why?* Positive word choice ("covenant," "promise," "better ordering," etc.) evokes positive emotions. Religious wording evokes reverence. The document begins by appealing to God and ends by referring to political authorities, emphasizing the seriousness of the covenant.

- **Ethos/Techniques/Structure:**
  - *How does Bradford establish credibility and trust? Where are these appeals and why?* The document is signed under the name of God and King James (these authority references enhance the credibility). These are placed at the beginning and end of the document to establish credibility.

Implications:
- *What are the implications of this document?* It set the precedent for future self-governing ideas.

Evaluation:
- *How effective is the author in supporting his claim?* The document could possibly pose more reasoning (logos) for self-government.

In-Class Activity to Deepen Learning

Using Handout 7.3: Reasoning About a Situation or Event, guide students in addressing the issue "Should the passengers sign the compact?" Students should reason through supporter and dissenter stakeholder perspectives.

Concept Connections

Lead students through a discussion using Handout 1.3: Concept Organizer. Students should list examples about how the work demonstrates some of the generalizations. Provide guidance as needed. Figure 7.1 provides some sample responses.

Choice-Based Differentiation Products

Students may choose one of the following independent products to complete (*Note*: Use Rubric 1: Product Rubric in Appendix C to assess student products):

- Write a first person narrative from the perspective of a Mayflower passenger. Base your narrative from an actual passenger on the *Mayflower*. Conduct basic background information about the individual to develop your story. In your narrative, reveal an internal conflict of whether to sign the compact or not. Include textual evidence from The Mayflower Compact in your narrative as you frame your story around your decision.
- Compare the Declaration of Independence or Pledge of Allegiance to The Mayflower Compact. Complete a comparison chart of at least four features to show similarities between the two documents. Include textual evidence in your chart (see Figure 7.2 for an example).
- Use multiple sources (including at least one primary source) to learn more about the passengers and purpose of the *Mayflower* voyage. Develop a fact or fiction presentation with 10 statements (e.g., Fact or fiction? All passengers on the *Mayflower* were pilgrims. Fiction: explain the facts). Present your findings to the class and explain how this information may be helpful in interpreting the context of The Mayflower Compact. Be sure to make connections to social conformity in your presentation.

| Both conformity and individuality are agents of change. |
| In binding together as a group (conforming and giving up individual differences), they set the stage for self-government and cooperation. |
| Both conformity and individuality involve sacrifice. |
| In binding together in social conformity, they put aside individual differences; those who did not sign do not benefit nor have protection from the covenant written. |
| There are positives and negatives to both conformity and individuality. |
| In conforming to the group, individuals benefit from a civil society. In conforming to the group, individuals may have to make personal sacrifices for the group. |
| Examine the relationship between conformity, individuality, and another related concept. |
| Students may relate concepts to freedom, government, and/or protection. |

Figure 7.1. Sample student responses to individuality versus conformity generalizations.

The Mayflower Compact Evidence	Similarities Explained	Second Document Evidence

Figure 7.2. Sample comparison chart.

Central Idea and Evidence	
0	Provides no response.
1	Response is limited, vague, and/or inaccurate. Only the central idea is mentioned with little support.
2	Response lacks adequate explanation. Some parts of the response are correct, but the response only vaguely addresses the author's central idea and evidence. Response lacks support.
3	Response is accurate and makes sense. Response includes 1–2 examples of support for the central idea.
4	Response is accurate, insightful, and well written. Response includes 2–3 examples of support for the central idea with textual evidence.

Figure 7.3. Scoring guidelines for Lesson 7 formative assessment.

ELA Practice Tasks

Assign one of the following tasks as a performance-based assessment for this lesson:

- In a well-developed essay, explain how The Mayflower Compact addresses both individuality and conformity at the same time. Develop an argument for which idea is supported most strongly. Support your argument claim with sufficient textual evidence. (Hint: They are acting as nonconformists from their old society because they are planting the first colony; they are conforming to the values of their new society.)
- How did The Mayflower Compact influence the idea of self-government in America? Using specific evidence from The Mayflower Compact and at least two other sources, develop a short research paper addressing the question. Cite your sources appropriately.

Formative Assessment

1. Ask students to respond to the following prompt in a single paragraph: *What is the central idea in The Mayflower Compact and how is it developed?*
2. Use the scoring guidelines in Figure 7.3 to evaluate students' assessments.

Handout 7.1
The Mayflower Compact

In the name of God, Amen. We whose names are underwritten, the loyal subjects of our dread Sovereign Lord King James, by the Grace of God of Great Britain, France, and Ireland King, Defender of the Faith, etc.

Having undertaken for the Glory of God and advancement of the Christian Faith and Honour of our King and Country, a Voyage to plant the First Colony in the Northern Parts of Virginia, do by these presents solemnly and mutually in the presence of God and one of another, Covenant and Combine ourselves together in a Civil Body Politic, for our better ordering and preservation and furtherance of the ends aforesaid; and by virtue hereof to enact, constitute and frame such just and equal Laws, Ordinances, Acts, Constitutions and Offices from time to time, as shall be thought most meet and convenient for the general good of the Colony, unto which we promise all due submission and obedience. In witness whereof we have hereunder subscribed our names at Cape Cod, the 11th of November, in the year of the reign of our Sovereign Lord King James, of England, France and Ireland the eighteenth, and of Scotland the fifty-fourth. Anno Domini 1620.

John Carver	Edward Tilley	Degory Priest
William Bradford	John Tilley	Thomas Williams
Edward Winslow	Francis Cooke	Gilbert Winslow
William Brewster	Thomas Rogers	Edmund Margeson
Issac Allerton	Thomas Tinker	Peter Browne
Myles Standish	John Rigdale	Richard Britteridge
John Alden	Edward Fuller	George Soule
Samuel Fuller	John Turner	Richard Clarke
Christopher Martin	Francis Eaton	Richard Gardiner
William Mullins	James Chilton	John Allerton
William White	John Crackston	Thomas English
Richard Warren	John Billington	Edward Dotey
John Howland	Moses Fletcher	Edward Leister
Stephen Hopkins	John Goodman	

Name: _____ Date: _____

Handout 7.2
Blank Rhetorical Analysis Wheel

Directions: Draw arrows across elements to show connections.

Text: _____

Purpose/Context

Point of View

Logos

Techniques

Pathos

Claim

Ethos

Structure/
Organization

Implications

Evaluation

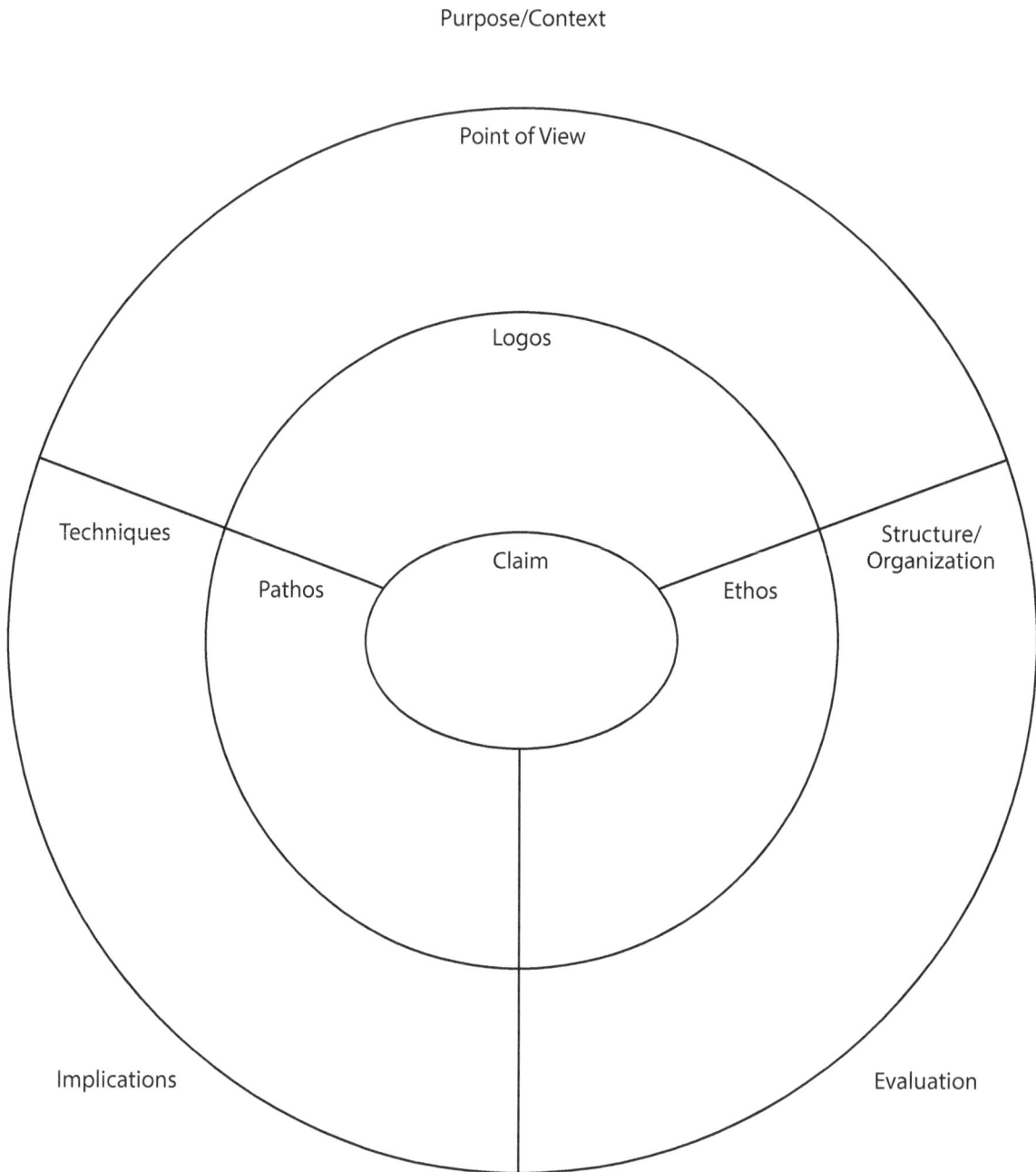

Created by Emily Mofield, Ed.D., & Tamra Stambaugh, Ph.D., 2015.

Handout 7.3
Reasoning About a Situation or Event

What Is the Situation?

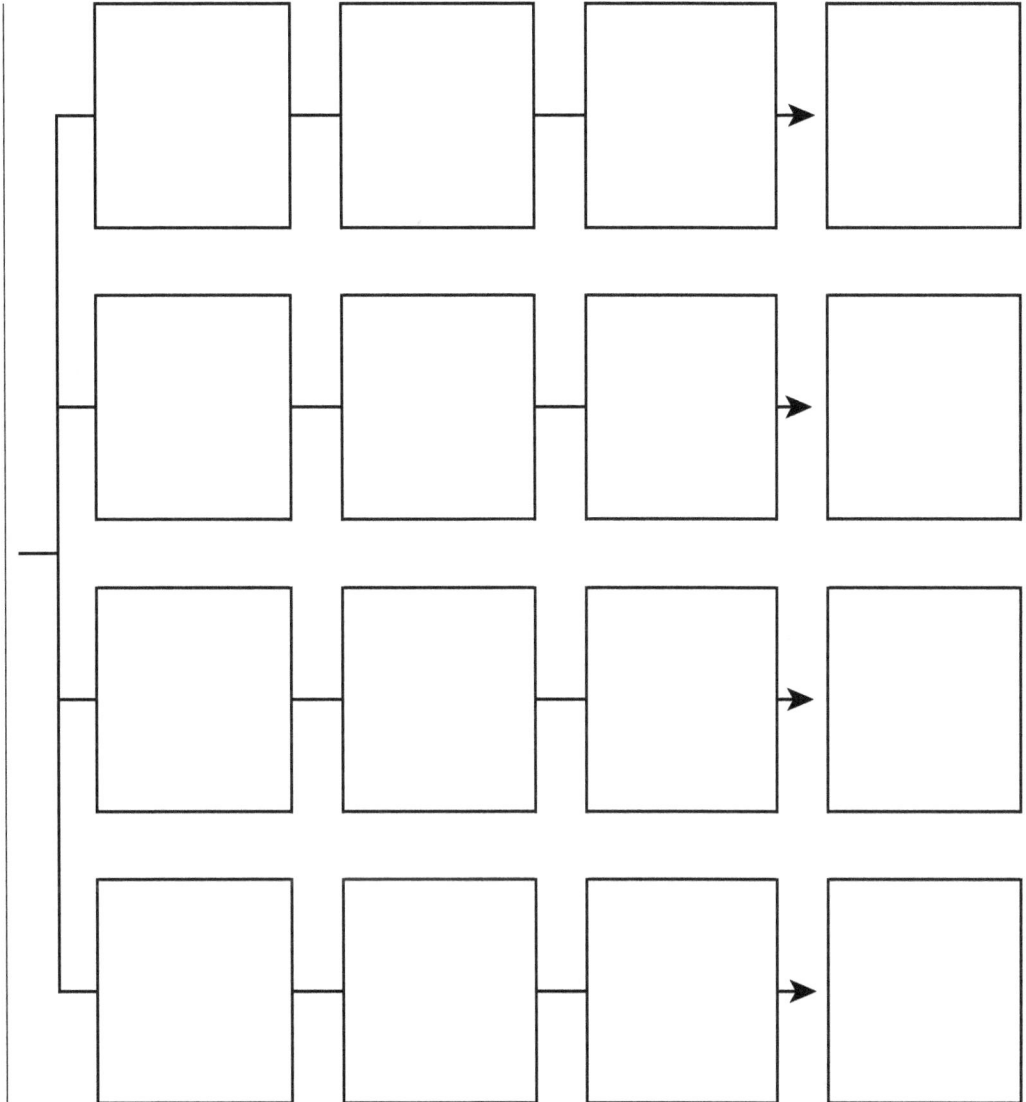

			→
			→
			→
			→

Stakeholders **Point of View** **Assumptions** **Implications**

Lesson

8

"Alone"
by Maya Angelou

Goals/Objectives

Content: To analyze and interpret texts and art, students will be able to:
- explain with evidence how literary and/or visual elements contribute to the overall meaning of a work,
- respond to interpretations of texts through a variety of contexts by justifying ideas and providing new information, and
- compare and contrast texts and real-world events on theme.

Process: To develop thinking, writing, and communication skills, students will be able to:
- use evidence to develop and support inferences, and
- analyze societal or individual conflicts resulting from the struggle between individuality versus conformity.

Concept: To understand the concept of individuality versus conformity in the language arts, students will be able to:
- support conformity versus individuality generalizations with evidence,
- develop and apply generalizations of additional key concepts, and
- explain the conflict between conformity and individuality.

Accelerated CCSS ELA Standards

RL.9-10.1	SL.9-10.1	SL.9-10.4
RL.9-10.2	SL.9-10.1c	W.9-10.4
RL.9-10.4	SL.9-10.1d	

Materials

- Student copies of "Alone" by Maya Angelou, available at http://www.poets.org/poetsorg/poem/alone

 DOI: 10.4324/9781003235620-14

- Handout 8.1: Blank Literary Analysis Wheel
- Handout 8.2: Big Idea Reflection
- Rubric 1: Product Rubric (Appendix C)

Note: This lesson addresses conformity and individuality from a different perspective. Conformity is related to the idea of belongingness and community (in being with others, one must conform in some ways to societal expectations), and individuality is related to the idea of isolation, a very extreme result of extreme individuality. Help students become *flexible* with their thinking when considering these concepts.

Introductory Activity

1. Provide a brief review. Ask: *Based on your learning in the unit thus far, when is conformity good? When is it bad?*
2. **Engage students in a quick debate.** Ask: *Agree or disagree?: It is possible to be happy and alone.* Students may discuss the issue by standing on opposite sides of the room to defend their points of view. Extend discussion by quantifying the statement (for 5 years, for 10 years, for the rest of one's life).

Read Text

Before distributing the poem, read aloud "Alone" by Maya Angelou. Ask students to draw images they associate with the poem. Students may also draw an abstract representation of the mood of the poem. Read the poem aloud at least twice. Ask students to share their drawings with a partner or the whole group. Ask students to explain how their drawing exemplifies the text. Then distribute or display "Alone" by Maya Angelou for students to read independently.

Text-Dependent Questions

Select from the following text-dependent questions for a Socratic seminar or class discussion:

- Does the poem offer a solution to isolation? How do you know? (*Note:* This is very debatable.)
- What is significant about the phrase, "where water is not thirsty?" Why would she personify water?
- Angelou writes, "Nobody can make it all alone." How would the wording "everyone needs somebody" change the tone of the poem? What is significant about the word choice "nobody?"

- Is the millionaire alone? How do you know? Why did she specifically mention this group?
- Where does the suffering in the poem originate?
- According to the poem, who suffers the most—the speaker or the millionaires?
- How do the first, third, and fifth stanzas show a shift in the speaker's ideas? (Sample response: At first she considers herself, then a specific group of people, then the world. Everyone suffers.)
- Is this poem about everyone or a certain group of people? How do you know?
- What is Angelou's attitude toward wealth?
- Is Angelou saying the world is getting better or worse? How do you know?
- What can we infer about the speaker's feelings about achieving happiness? Support your answer with textual evidence. (Sample response: It can't be achieved without other people, and money cannot buy it; what good is happiness if you can't share it with others?)

Literary Analysis

1. You may wish to consult an expert analysis of the poem (many are available online) before guiding student discussion. Guide students through a literary analysis using Handout 8.2: Blank Literary Analysis Wheel. Lead students through a basic discussion of each literary element, then emphasize the interaction of the elements with more complex questions. Encourage students to cite textual evidence throughout discussion. Students can take notes on the wheel and draw arrows to illustrate connections between concepts. Focus on the following complex questions:
   - How does the language shape the conflict in the poem?
   - How does the structure of the poem contribute to the theme?
   - How does Angelou's repetition of "nobody" contribute to the theme?

2. The following notes may be helpful in guiding students through the analysis:
   - **Themes:** Themes may relate to isolation, loneliness, social classes, and/ or suffering.
   - **Setting:** The setting of lying in bed allows the reader to realize that the speaker may be praying and soul-searching, realizing that the solution to isolation may not exist on Earth; speaking of millionaires shows that loneliness crosses all social barriers.
   - **Conflict:** Conflicts may include loneliness versus community, suffering versus peace.

- **Language/Structure:** Consider the chronological structure—at first she considers herself, then a specific group of people, then the world. Everyone suffers. Repetition of "alone" and "nobody" emphasizes the theme.
- **Point of View:** Angelou's point of view leads readers to consider the value of belongingness.
- **Context:** Provide historical background knowledge on the poem. This was written by Maya Angelou, an African American poet (1928–2014). The poem was first published in 1975.

Note: Elements of this analysis are adapted from "Alone Summary" by Shmoop Editorial Team, 2008, retrieved from http://www.shmoop.com/alone-angelou/summary.html.

Big Idea Reflection

Students can work with partners or in a small group to discuss the big ideas in the poem and relate them to real life. They may use Handout 8.3: Big Idea Reflection as a guide for discussion.

- **Concepts:** Community, isolation, suffering.
- **Generalizations:** What generalization about Conformity versus Individuality do you see as most evident in the story? What other generalizations can be made?
- **Problem:** Being alone, not knowing how to nourish the soul through community
- **Insight:** We all need community.
- **World/Community/Individual:** Individual—In what ways do I isolate myself? Will this hurt me? Why is the world more isolated today?
- **Solutions/Implications:** How might I personally respond to the issues within the poem? What are the implications of these ideas on my life?

In-Class Activities to Deepen Learning

1. **Engage students in a quick debate.** Revisit the opening debate: *Agree or disagree?: It is possible to be happy and alone. How would Angelou answer? How would another author/artist you have read/seen respond to this question?*
2. Hold a discussion. Ask: *Which character or person from previous unit lessons is most like the speaker in the poem "Alone"? Consider Mr. Bittering, Margot, Eleanor Roosevelt, Picasso, and the Mayflower passengers.*

3. Provide selected quotes from Maya Angelou and have students paraphrase and illustrate them. Students should also make a connection to the poem or any other lesson within the unit.

4. Have students develop a list of questions to ask Maya Angelou about the poem "Alone." Why did you . . . ? What did you mean by . . . ? If time remains, they can develop answers by researching about her background and imagining how she might answer.

Concept Connections

Discuss connections to individuality versus conformity by asking the following questions. Students may reflect on concept connections using Handout 1.3: Concept Organizer, continued from previous lessons. Figure 8.1 provides some sample responses.

- How is the idea of belongingness related to conformity? In what ways are these ideas different?
- Does conformity fulfill our need to belong?
- On the spectrum of conformity and individuality, where does Angelou think achieving happiness falls?
- In what ways is this poem not about conformity?
- What does Angelou say is dangerous about independence?

Choice-Based Differentiated Products

Students may choose one of the following independent products to complete (*Note*: Use Rubric 1: Product Rubric in Appendix C to assess student products):

- Rewrite the poem focusing on providing antonyms of key words. For example, instead of writing "alone" write "belonging" throughout. Change "nobody," to "everybody," etc. Note how this changes the tone of the poem. Rewrite the entire poem with applicable antonyms to either maintain the meaning of the poem or to reverse it. Provide an explanation of how word choice impacts the theme.
- Apply a Literary Analysis Wheel and Big Idea Reflection to another poem by Maya Angelou. Create a poem movie using Windows Movie Maker or similar software. Incorporate music, words, and images associated with the poem.
- Research more about the life of Maya Angelou using at least three different sources (one must be a primary source). Write a multiparagraph essay that shows how the poem "Alone" reflects Angelou's life experiences. Cite textual evidence from your research and the poem in your expository essay.

Both conformity and individuality are agents of change.
Extreme forms of individuality (being alone in this lesson) promote the need for community, which can provoke one to find community.
Both conformity and individuality involve sacrifice.
Extreme forms of individuality (being alone) can cause isolation and loneliness.
There are positives and negatives to both conformity and individuality.
Having community is positive and necessary; extreme individuality (being alone) causes one to miss the most important things in life.
Examine the relationship between conformity, individuality, and another related concept.
Students may consider concepts such as belongingness, isolation, happiness, and/or money.

Figure 8.1. Sample student responses to individuality versus conformity generalizations.

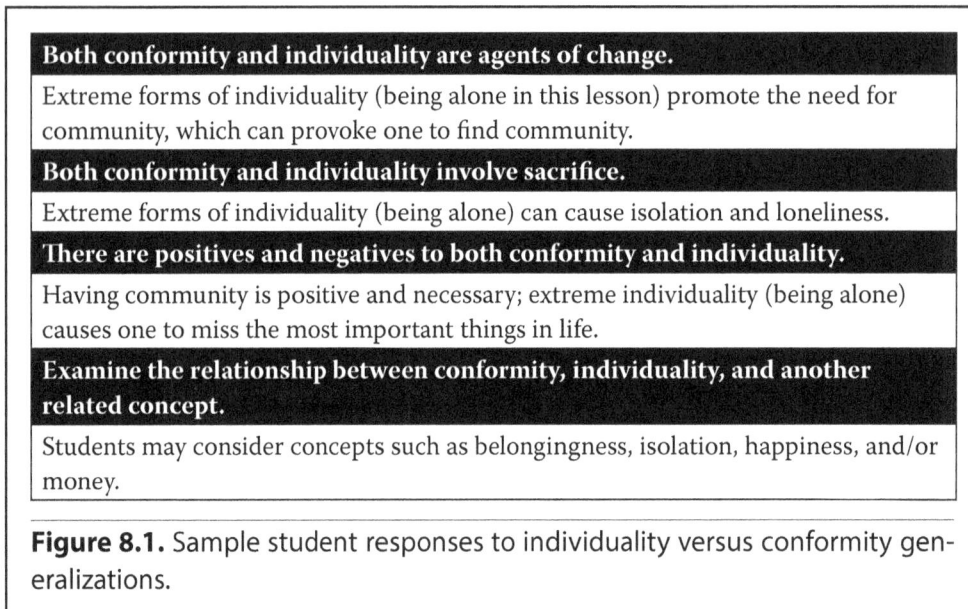

- Write your own poem about being alone or belonging. Apply the same structure of Angelou's poem (Verse A, Verse B, Verse C, Verse B, Verse D, Verse B) and use figurative language.

ELA Practice Tasks

Assign one of the following tasks as a performance-based assessment for this lesson:

- In a well-developed essay, describe how Angelou develops the theme of isolation in the poem "Alone." Cite relevant evidence from the poem referring to literary techniques to develop your response.
- Does the poem offer a solution to isolation? In an essay, develop your argument by supporting your claim with relevant and sufficient evidence from the poem.
- Which character or person from previous unit lessons is most like the speaker in the poem "Alone"? Consider Mr. Bittering, Margot, Eleanor Roosevelt, Picasso, and the Mayflower passengers. Write an essay in which you develop your argument, citing evidence from the poem and a previous text in this unit to support your claim.

	Claim/Message and Evidence
0	Provides no response.
1	Response is limited, vague, and/or inaccurate. Only the message is mentioned with little support.
2	Response lacks adequate explanation. Some parts of the response are correct, but the response only vaguely addresses the author's message and evidence. Response lacks support.
3	Response is accurate and makes sense. Response includes 1–2 examples of support for the message.
4	Response is accurate, insightful, and well written. Response includes 2–3 examples of support for the message with textual evidence.

Figure 8.2. Scoring guidelines for Lesson 8 formative assessment.

Formative Assessment

1. Ask students to respond to the following prompt in a single paragraph: *What is Angelou's main message in her poem, and how is it supported? Cite textual evidence.*

2. Use the scoring guidelines in Figure 8.2 to evaluate students' assessments.

Name: _____ Date: _____

Handout 8.1

Blank Literary Analysis Wheel

Directions: Draw arrows across elements to show connections.

Text: _____

Purpose/Context

Setting

Language
Structure
Style

Symbols

Mood

Plot/
Conflict

Characters

Theme

Point of View

Tone

Interpretation

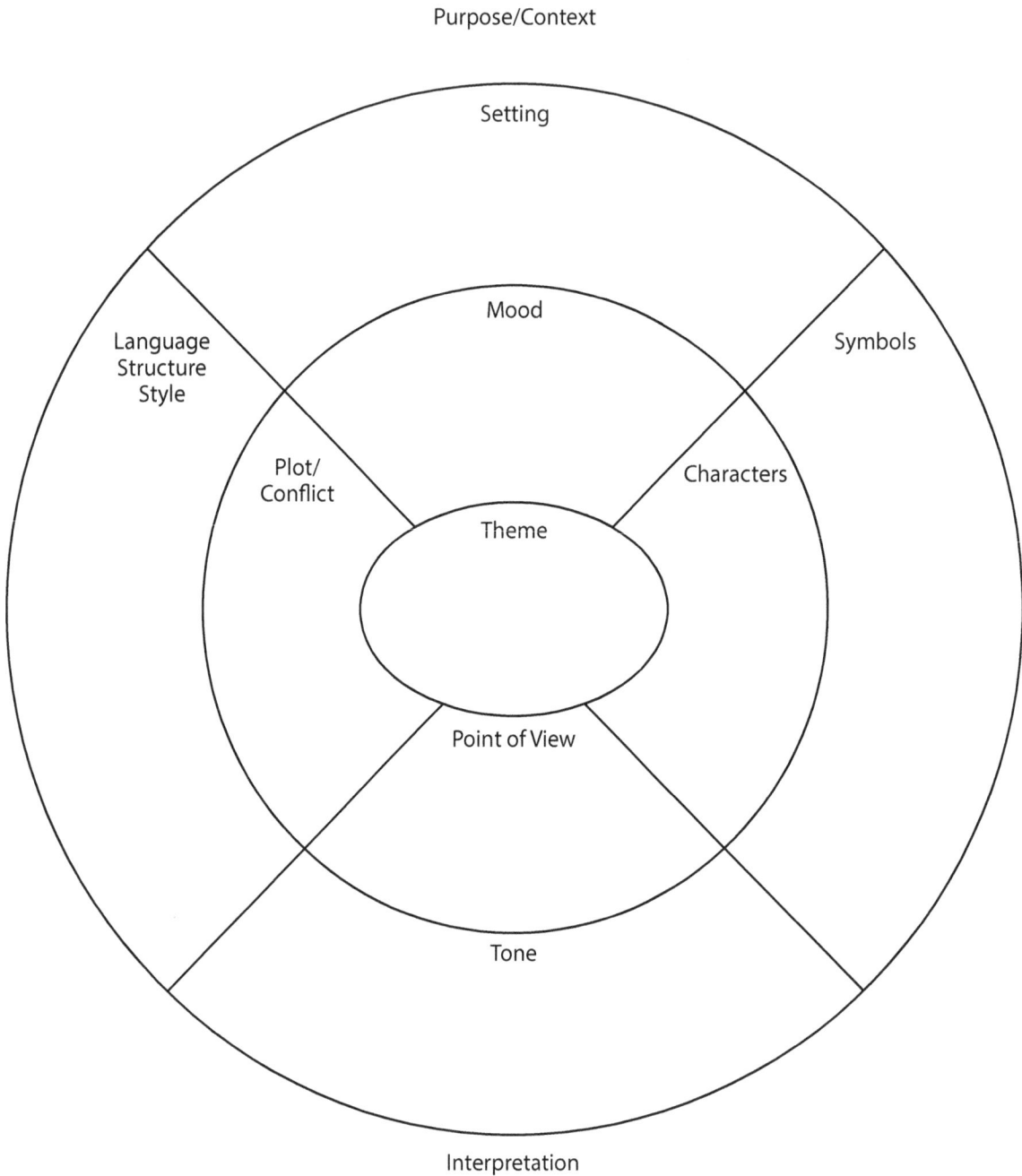

Created by Tamra Stambaugh, Ph.D., & Emily Mofield, Ed.D., 2015.

Name: _____ Date: _____

Handout 8.2
Big Idea Reflection

What?	**Concepts:** What concepts/ideas are in the text?	
	Generalizations: What broad statement can you make about one or more of these concepts? Make it generalizable beyond the text.	
	Issue: What is the main issue, problem, or conflict?	
So What?	**Insight:** What insight on life is provided from this text?	
	World/Community/Individual: How does this text relate to you, your community, or your world? What question does the author want you to ask yourself?	
Now What?	**Implications:** How should you respond to the ideas in the text? What action should you take? What are the implications of the text? What can you do with this information?	

Created by Emily Mofield, Ed.D., & Tamra Stambaugh, Ph.D., 2015.

Lesson

9

"Harrison Bergeron"
by Kurt Vonnegut

Goals/Objectives

Content: To analyze and interpret texts and art, students will be able to:
- explain with evidence how literary and/or visual elements contribute to the overall meaning of a work,
- respond to interpretations of texts through a variety of contexts by justifying ideas and providing new information, and
- compare and contrast texts and real-world events on theme.

Process: To develop thinking, writing, and communication skills, students will be able to:
- use evidence to develop and support inferences, and
- analyze societal or individual conflicts resulting from the struggle between individuality versus conformity.

Concept: To understand the concept of individuality versus conformity in the language arts, students will be able to:
- support conformity versus individuality generalizations with evidence,
- develop and apply generalizations of additional key concepts, and
- explain the conflict between conformity and individuality.

Accelerated CCSS ELA Standards

RL.9-10.1	RL.9-10.4	SL.9-10.1d
RL.9-10.2	SL.9-10.1	SL.9-10.4
RL.9-10.3	SL.9-10.1c	W.9-10.4

Materials

- Student copies of "Harrison Bergeron" by Kurt Vonnegut, available at http://www.tnellen.com/westside/harrison.pdf

 DOI: 10.4324/9781003235620-15

Handout 9.1: Blank Literary Analysis Wheel
Handout 9.2: Big Idea Reflection
Handout 9.3: Reasoning About a Situation or Event
Rubric 1: Product Rubric (Appendix C)
Rubric 2: Collage Rubric (Appendix C)

Note: Use the stories with discretion as they involve an act of execution. You may choose to substitute another text and use the same questioning models and organizer.

Introductory Activities

1. Ask students to define *equality*. Ask students in groups draw a picture or sculpt the term *equality*.
2. Ask students to respond to the following in a quick write: *When do individual freedoms come in conflict with society as a whole?*
3. **Engage students in a quick debate.** Students may stand on opposite sides of the room to explain their reasoning regarding the following statements. *Agree or disagree?*
    Fair means the same treatment for all.
    Equal means same.

4. Hold a discussion. Ask: *How can individuals be treated equally when we are all different? Would treating everyone equally have positive or negative consequences?*

Read Text

Distribute copies of "Harrison Bergeron" by Kurt Vonnegut. Students may read the text independently or you may conduct a scaled-down version of reader's theater. Students will read those parts of the story aloud. Though the story is not written as a play, it can still be read in parts if the students are savvy about following along and understand the dialogue.
    Narrator
    George
    Hazel
    Ms. Glampers
    Ballerina
    Harrison Bergeron

Text-Dependent Questions

Select from the following text-dependent questions for a Socratic seminar or class discussion:

- What inferences can we make about the society depicted in "Harrison Bergeron"? How does it promote equality?
- What effect does the clammy month of April have on the story's mood and overall meaning?
- Why does the author emphasize details about George and Hazel's intelligence? What effect does this have on the story?
- According to the text, what happened in the "dark ages"? What effect would this have on society?
- Why did Vonnegut include a person with a speech impediment as the television announcer? What effect do Vonnegut's exaggerations in his story have on the story's message? (Sample response: He is making fun of contemporary society—this story is satirical.)
- Categorize the noises used throughout the text. Do they promote action or inaction for George? Why is this important to the overall message of the story? (Sample response: Vonnegut is speaking about the tendency for individuals to watch crises on television but take no action to help.)
- What do the weights symbolize? How do you know? (Sample response: Oppression.)
- What is meant by the narrator in stating, "She must have been extraordinarily beautiful because the mask she wore was hideous"? Note Vonnegut's use of satire—characters wear different masks, but not the same masks, so they are not truly equal.
- Is Harrison a hero or a rebel? Support your answer with evidence.
- How does Vonnegut contrast character perspectives?
- What effect does the simple dialogue have on the story?
- How would this story be different if it did not take place in the future? How would this affect the overall message?
- What specific parts of the story poke fun at contemporary society?
- Additional questions to promote thinking (optional):
  - Is legal always right?
  - Why would a society make things that are *different* illegal? What would be the motivation?
  - Under what circumstance should conscience supersede the law?

Literary Analysis

In small groups, students should work through a literary analysis using Handout 9.1: Blank Literary Analysis Wheel. Students may focus on each literary element, then explore the interaction of the elements. Encourage students to cite textual evidence throughout discussion. Students can take notes on the wheel and draw arrows to illustrate connections between concepts. Focus on the following complex questions as a whole group:

- Why is the future setting important in understanding the theme?
- How does the characterization of Harrison Bergeron contribute to the conflict?
- How do the characters' reactions to conflict influence our understanding of each character's values and motives?
- How does the style of the author (e.g., exaggeration, satire) contribute to the development of theme?

Big Idea Reflection

(Optional) Students can work with partners or in a small group to discuss the big ideas in the story and relate them to real life. They may use Handout 9.2: Big Idea Reflection as a guide for discussion.

In-Class Activities to Deepen Learning

1. (Optional) Ask students to compare a dystopian novel/movie they have read/ watched (e.g., Hunger Games series, Divergent series, Maze Runner series) to "Harrison Bergeron." Students can make comparisons about the texts (see Figure 9.1. for an example chart).

2. Evaluate the issue "Is Harrison Bergeron a hero?" by guiding students through a discussion using Handout 9.3: Reasoning About a Situation or Event.
    - **Point of View:** How the stakeholder(s) would answer the question, including evidence of why they feel this way.
    - **Assumptions:** The values and beliefs taken for granted by the stakeholders.
    - **Implications:** The short- and long-term consequences that happened or could have happened if that particular point of view were actualized.

3. Have students read a current event article that shows how the government works to protect its people but may limit personal freedoms at the same time. Have students debate both sides in groups and then discuss their selected issue's relevance to the short story.

	"Harrison Bergeron"	Similarities	Student Choice
Theme			
Setting			
Characters			
Conflict			
Tone			

Figure 9.1. Sample comparison chart.

Concept Connections

Discuss connections to individuality versus conformity by asking the following questions. Students may reflect on concept connections using Handout 1.3: Concept Organizer, continued from previous lessons. Figure 9.2 provides some sample responses.

- How is rebellion related to individuality and conformity?
- What are the positives to conformity, as revealed in the story?
- How was Harrison Bergeron an agent for change?

Choice-Based Differentiated Products

Students may choose one of the following independent products to complete (*Note*: Use Rubric 1: Product Rubric in Appendix C to assess student products):

- Think about the reasons why the government in "Harrison Bergeron" acts the way they do. Rewrite the short story from first person or third person limited from the view of the government officials. Reveal insight into the motivations of the government and the need for so many additional amendments.
- Research Kurt Vonnegut's political ideas and motivations for this story. How would Kurt Vonnegut feel about recent contemporary societal issues? Present your findings in an essay and oral presentation.

| **Both conformity and individuality are agents of change.** |
| Harrison Bergeron's rebellion presented a major change in the daily routine within the 2081 societal context. |
| **Both conformity and individuality involve sacrifice.** |
| Harrison Bergeron sacrificed his life in his rebellion. |
| **There are positives and negatives to both conformity and individuality.** |
| Those who conform in this society are safe but are controlled. Those who show their true individuality risk their lives. |
| **Examine the relationship between conformity, individuality, and another related concept.** |
| Students may consider the relationship between individuality, identity, fear, equality, conformity, power, oppression, and freedom. |

Figure 9.2. Sample student responses to individuality versus conformity generalizations.

- Write a dialogue between Harrison Bergeron and another character or person in this unit. Create the dialogue so that the characters both agree and disagree on various points about conformity and individuality. Characters should support their responses with experiences with textual evidence.
- Think of how you see elements of "Harrison Bergeron" in today's world. Create a visual collage with quotes, words, newspaper articles, and pictures to reveal these similarities. Turn in your collage as well as a written description of the elements on your collage and how they relate to "Harrison Bergeron." Use specific examples from the story to support your symbols in explaining how our world and "Harrison Bergeron" are the same and different (see Rubric 2: Collage Rubric, Appendix C).

ELA Practice Tasks

Assign one of the following tasks as a performance-based assessment for this lesson:

- What is Vonnegut's message about equality? In a well-developed essay, address the question using relevant evidence from the story "Harrison Bergeron."
- After reading "Harrison Bergeron" by Kurt Vonnegut and another dystopian story, write an essay that compares how the theme of individuality is developed in each.

	Concept/Theme
0	Provides no response.
1	Response is limited, vague, and/or inaccurate.
2	Response lacks adequate explanation. Response does not relate or create a generalization about individuality versus conformity. Little or no evidence from text.
3	Response is accurate and makes sense. Response relates to or creates an idea about individuality versus conformity with some relation to the text.
4	Response is accurate, insightful, and well written. Response relates to or creates a generalization about individuality versus conformity with evidence from the text.

Figure 9.3. Scoring guidelines for Lesson 9 formative assessment.

Formative Assessment

1. Ask students to respond to the following prompt in a single paragraph: *What does this text reveal about the big idea of individuality versus conformity? Be sure to relate to generalizations in your response.*
2. Use the scoring guidelines in Figure 9.3 to evaluate students' assessments.

Name: _____ Date: _____

Handout 9.1

Blank Literary Analysis Wheel

Directions: Draw arrows across elements to show connections.

Text: _____

Purpose/Context

Setting

Mood

Language
Structure
Style

Symbols

Plot/
Conflict

Characters

Theme

Point of View

Tone

Interpretation

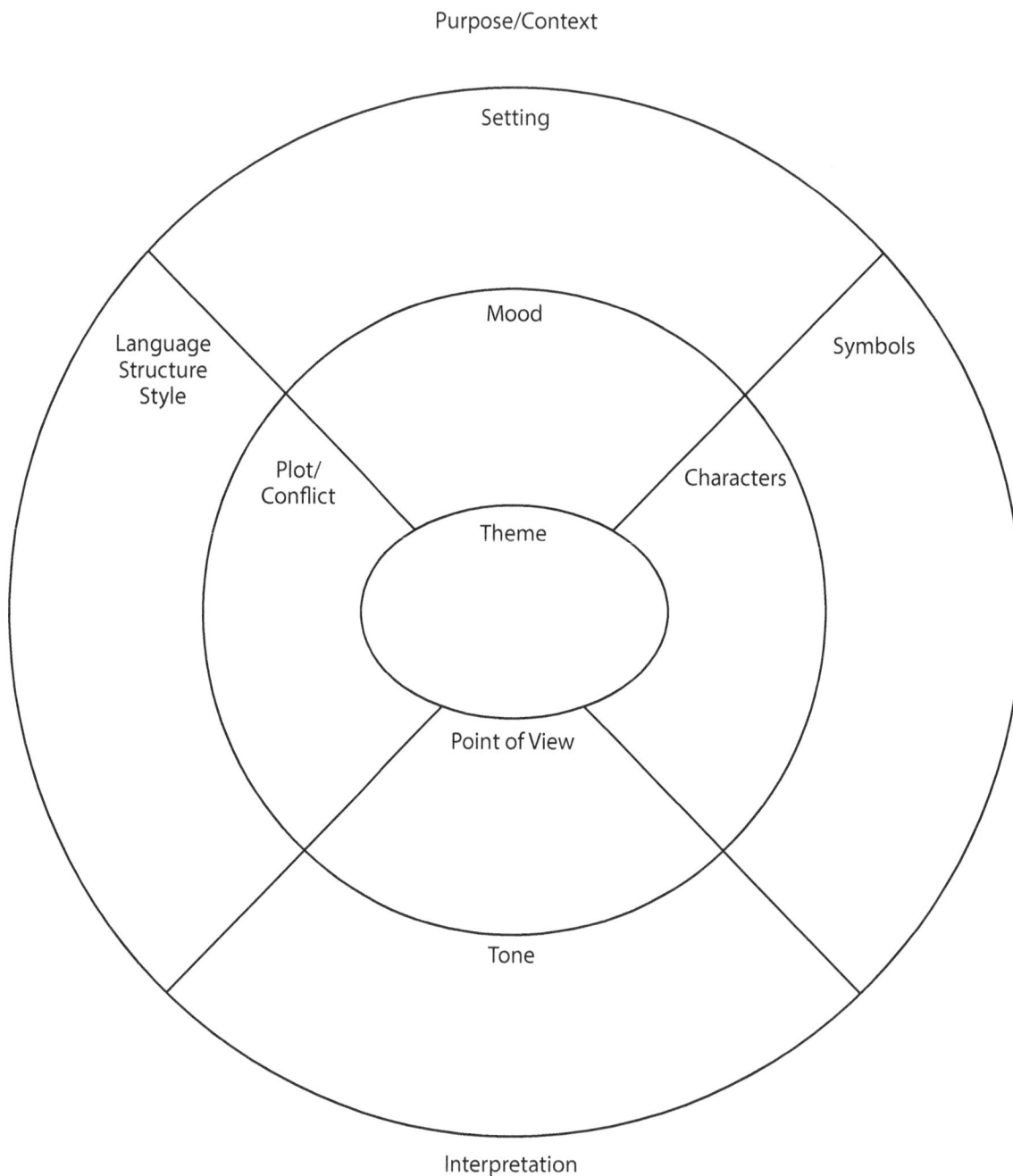

Created by Tamra Stambaugh, Ph.D., & Emily Mofield, Ed.D., 2015.

I, Me, You, We © Taylor & Francis

Name: _____ Date: _____

Handout 9.2
Big Idea Reflection

What?	**Concepts:** What concepts/ideas are in the text?	
	Generalizations: What broad statement can you make about one or more of these concepts? Make it generalizable beyond the text.	
	Issue: What is the main issue, problem, or conflict?	
So What?	**Insight:** What insight on life is provided from this text?	
	World/Community/Individual: How does this text relate to you, your community, or your world? What question does the author want you to ask yourself?	
Now What?	**Implications:** How should you respond to the ideas in the text? What action should you take? What are the implications of the text? What can you do with this information?	

Created by Emily Mofield, Ed.D., & Tamra Stambaugh, Ph.D., 2015.

Handout 9.3

Reasoning About a Situation or Event

What Is the Situation?

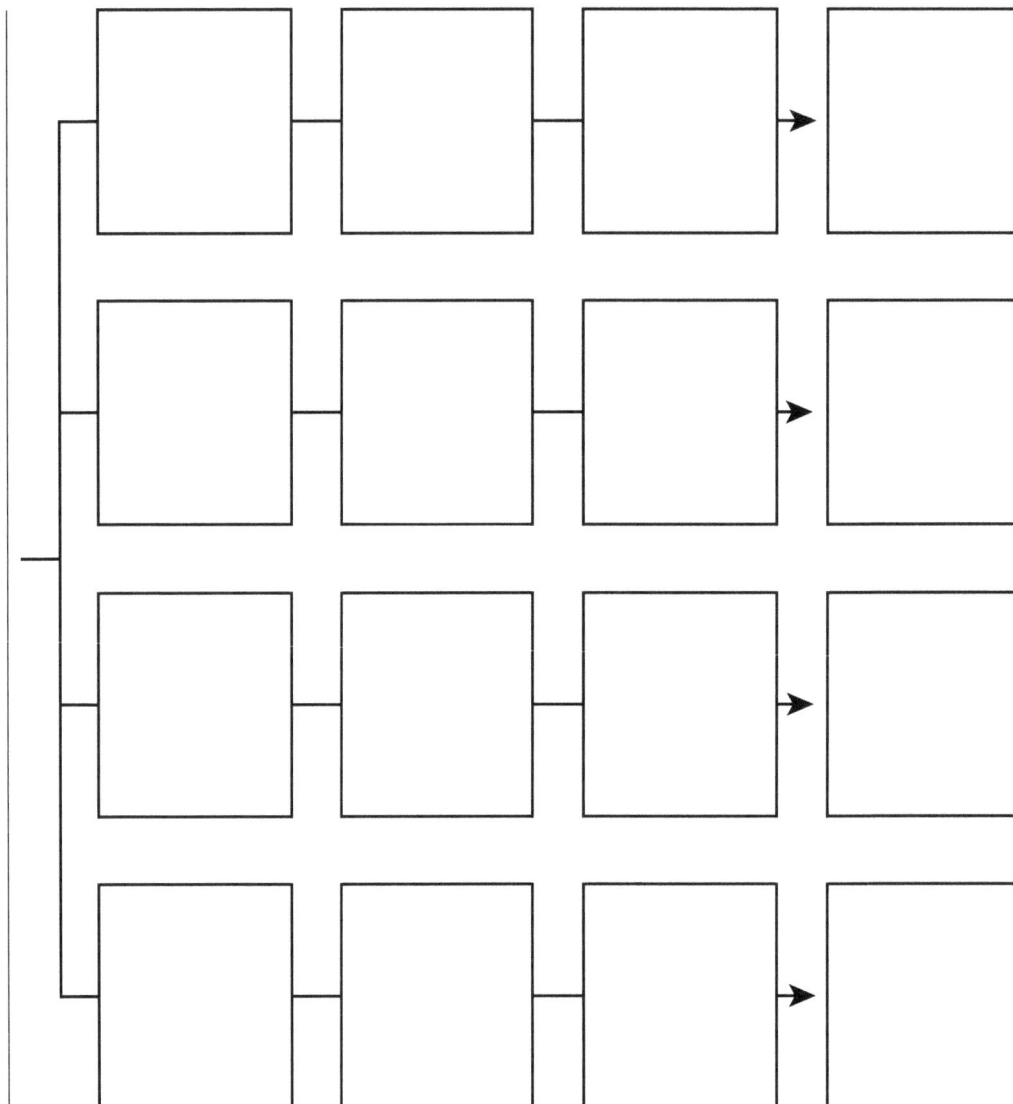

Stakeholders

Point of View

Assumptions

Implications

AN EXAMINATION OF NONCONFORMITY

A Force of Social Change

DOI: 10.4324/9781003235620-16

Lesson

Excerpts From "Self-Reliance"
by Ralph Waldo Emerson

Goals/Objectives

Content: To analyze and interpret texts and art, students will be able to:
- explain with evidence how a writer supports a claim,
- respond to interpretations of texts through a variety of contexts by justifying ideas and providing new information,
- compare and contrast texts and real-world events on theme, and
- evaluate rhetoric within primary sources.

Process: To develop thinking, writing, and communication skills, students will be able to:
- use evidence to develop and support inferences,
- evaluate the use of effective argumentation, and
- analyze societal or individual conflicts resulting from the struggle between individuality versus conformity.

Concept: To understand the concept of individuality versus conformity in the language arts, students will be able to:
- support conformity versus individuality generalizations with evidence,
- develop and apply generalizations of additional key concepts, and
- explain the conflict between conformity and individuality.

Accelerated CCSS ELA Standards

RI.9-10.1	SL.9-10.1	RH.9-10.8
RI.9-10.2	SL.9-10.1c	RH.9-10.9
RI.9-10.3	SL.9-10.1d	W.9-10.4
RI.9-10.4	RH.9-10.1	
RI.9-10.5	RH.9-10.2	
RI.9-10.6	RH.9-10.5	
RI.9-10.9	RH.9-10.4	

 DOI: 10.4324/9781003235620-17

Materials

- Handout 1.3: Concept Organizer
- Handout 10.1: Excerpts From "Self-Reliance" by Ralph Waldo Emerson
- Handout 10.2: Selected Quote (consider using if the longer excerpt is too difficult)
- Handout 10.3: Blank Rhetorical Analysis Wheel
- Rubric 1: Product Rubric (Appendix C)

Introductory Activities

1. Divide students into groups based on readiness. Assign each group to do a small amount of research on one of the following topics about Ralph Waldo Emerson:
    - His childhood
    - People who influenced him
    - The movement of Transcendentalism
    - His views about current events during his time (e.g., slavery)
    - His jobs
    - Information about his books/essays
    - His influence on Henry David Thoreau and others

2. Conduct a jigsaw activity to allow students to share their findings with others who have investigated a different topic. Discuss findings as a class.
3. Ask: *How would you define self-reliance? Would you say it is the same as independence? How is it different from individuality, or is it?* Explain that students will be reading an essay in which Emerson defines this concept.

Read Text

Distribute Handout 10.1: Excerpts From "Self-Reliance" by Ralph Waldo Emerson. Ask students to highlight quotes they think are important as it is read. Encourage students to read first independently, then read as a group, a paragraph at time. This can be a difficult first read. If the text is too difficult, consider focusing the lesson on Handout 10.2: Selected Quote in forthcoming sections of the lesson.

Text-Dependent Questions

Select from the following text-dependent questions for a Socratic seminar or class discussion about the excerpts from "Self-Reliance":

- Emerson mentions "genius" twice in the first paragraph. How does he define genius and what do we recognize within the genius?
- Why does Emerson refer to Moses, Plato, and Milton as geniuses? How does this support the main idea of this paragraph?
- What is meant by "envy is ignorance" and "imitation is suicide"?
- Reword "Trust thyself . . . connection of events" in your own words.
- Why is it significant that Emerson refers to great men as "childlike"?
- What pattern does Emerson develop in the last few sentences of the paragraph beginning with "Trust thyself . . . "? (Sample response: He develops contrasts between minors, cowards, invalids and guides, redeemers and benefactors.)
- Who are the minors, invalids, and cowards? Who are the guides, redeemers, and benefactors? (Sample response: He is talking about conformists and nonconformists, respectively.) Why are these words important to Emerson's development of self-reliance?
- "Society everywhere is in conspiracy against the manhood of every one of its members." What point is Emerson making and what effect does it have on the reader?
- What two contrasting concepts are presented in the last few sentences in the paragraph beginning with "These are the various voices . . . "? (Sample response: Self-reliance versus conformity.)
- How does Emerson define self-reliance? What words does he associate with self-reliance and what words does he associate with society? How does this contrast help develop his definition of self-reliance?

Rhetorical Analysis

In small groups or in whole group, have students complete the Handout 10.3: Blank Rhetorical Analysis Wheel through guided discussion of text. Emphasize specific elements first (e.g., logos, pathos, ethos, organization, techniques, and point of view), then move toward combining elements for more complexity (e.g., what techniques does he use to develop pathos appeals; where are they placed and why?). Sample questions to lead analysis include:

- **Context/Purpose:**
  - *What is the historical context?* It was written in 1841—Emerson is influenced by the Abolitionist Movement. He is one of the key Transcendentalist authors.
  - *What is Emerson's purpose?* To encourage others to avoid conformity and embrace the power within (inner voice).

Claim:

- *What is Emerson's main claim?* Trust the genius within yourself rather than society.

Point of View/Assumptions:

- *What is Emerson's point of view? What are his assumptions?* Emerson speaks from a Transcendentalist perspective—an individualistic philosophy. His key belief is that there is inherent goodness in the individual.

Logos/Techniques/Structure:

- *What are Emerson's main points?* Major points in this excerpt are about the self-contained genius and the disapproval of society: Speak conviction. Work with what you have been given. Don't be a coward—transcend to your destiny. Follow your voice rather than society.
- *How does structure help develop these points?* He starts out by giving examples of nonconformists and ends by explaining the difficulty of being in society.
- *What techniques does he use to develop his rationale? Why are these techniques used?* He uses allusions to Plato, Moses, and Milton to develop the point of speaking with conviction. He uses the metaphor of a corn kernel to develop his point to work with what you have been given. He uses contrasts of cowards and redeemers to develop his point of advancing to transcendent destiny. He uses the metaphor that society is a joint-stock company to explain the difficulty of being in society.

Pathos/Techniques:

- *How does Emerson develop emotional appeals?* He uses positive connotations of words throughout (e.g., "transcend destiny," "great men," "advancing on Chaos and the Dark," "sacred . . . integrity of your own mind") to develop inspiration in the readers.

Ethos/Techniques/Structure:

- *How does Emerson develop credibility?* He has been inspired by thoughts from "an eminent painter"—a credible source. He establishes a connection with the reader using "us" and "we": "And we are now men . . . " (also developing a pathos appeal).

Implications:

- *What are the short- and long-term implications/consequences of this document?* It influenced Thoreau. Ideas of Transcendentalism and individualism spread, causing people to question society's traditions of conformity.

Evaluation:

- *How effective is the author in supporting his claim?* Emerson eloquently develops the claim to trust the genius in you through the way he develops his points. He evokes an emotional reaction in the reader through his inspiring word choice.

Read Text

If Handout 10.1 is too difficult, then focus the lesson on Handout 10.2: Selected Quote. This can also be read as an addition to the longer excerpt. This selected quote is from Emerson's latter part of his essay "Self-Reliance." Students may need to read it several times to gain understanding.

Note: In the context of Handout 10.2, consistency refers to doing the same thing over and over again without questioning it. It means doing something because everyone else may be doing it. We often choose to be "foolish" in compromising our true selves when we are overly influenced by society.

In-Class Activities to Deepen Learning

1. Ask students to read through the excerpt (Handout 10.1) and find five significant meaningful quotes. Have students rewrite the quotes as bumper stickers, slogans, or text messages with emojis.
2. Ask students to choose one sentence from the excerpt or quote, rewrite it in their own words, and draw a picture to show its meaning. Students can also develop a tableau pose for the quote (tableau: a group of motionless figures to represent an idea).
3. Referring to Handout 10.2: Selected Quote, play a song relevant to "the genius within" such as Katy Perry's "Firework." Have students make connections between the song and Emerson's excerpts.
4. Assign students a letter of Emerson's (first or last) name (e.g., R, W, E, etc.). Have students write the letter on their paper and create a visual to depict their interpretation of the excerpt, using the letter as the basic foundation of their drawing. For example, if a student draws a giant W and makes the W into mountains, he or she could draw the individual at the top of the mountain and society at the bottom. The individual has realized his greatness.

5. Have students develop a song/musical interpretation of the text. Just as many contemporary musicians have developed music relevant to this topic, invite students to do so by incorporating Emerson's specific ideas.
6. You may wish to help students make personal connections to the selected quote ("A foolish consistency . . . "). Students may come to the understanding that when they are in their comfort zones of "consistency" no risk is taken. Gifted students may avoid risk-taking to avoid failure in order to maintain an identity of being smart or even "perfect."

Concept Connections

Lead students through a discussion, using Handout 1.3: Concept Organizer (continued from previous lessons). Ask: *How are these generalizations exemplified in Emerson's text?* Students should list examples about how the work demonstrates some of these generalizations. Provide guidance as needed. Figure 10.1 provides some sample responses.

Choice-Based Differentiated Products

Students may choose one of the following independent products to complete (*Note*: Use Rubric 1: Product Rubric in Appendix C to assess student products):

- Research more about Emerson's life. Conduct a mock interview with Ralph Waldo Emerson. Develop questions pertaining to how his life influenced the development of his essay, "Self-Reliance."
- How would Emerson feel about a contemporary issue in America today? Using evidence from his essay, "Self-Reliance," write an expository essay explaining how he would feel about the issue and what he would encourage others to do.
- Find examples of ideas in "Self-Reliance" in media, books, newspapers, and music. Find at least five examples and explain how they exemplify Emerson's idea in a multimedia presentation. Cite evidence from Emerson's text to support your answer.
- To what parts of Emerson's essay do you agree and disagree? Explain your thinking in a multiparagraph essay or a presentation to your peers. Cite the specific quotes in which you agree and disagree in your response.
- Research more about the Transcendental movement, referring to at least one other primary source document. In a multimedia presentation, teach the class about the basics behind this philosophy and how we see its effects today. Be sure a part of your presentation addresses the individuality versus conformity theme.

Both conformity and individuality are agents of change.
Individuals have power within themselves to be geniuses and change the world with their individual values or ideas.
Both conformity and individuality involve sacrifice.
Individuals must advance through chaos and the dark. Society may conspire against us, but we have to trust the self-contained genius within.
There are positives and negatives to both conformity and individuality.
Positive: If we are true to ourselves, then we can be great like Moses, Plato, and Milton, who spoke not what men thought, but what they thought. Negative: Our inner voices become faint as we enter the world/society.
Examine the relationship between conformity, individuality, and another related concept.
Students may consider the relationship between individuality, conformity, power, oppression, and freedom.

Figure 10.1. *How are these generalizations exemplified in Emerson's text?* Sample responses.

ELA Practice Tasks

Assign one of the following tasks as a performance-based assessment for this lesson:

- In an expository essay, explain how Emerson defines a "nonconformist" within the excerpt from "Self-Reliance." Cite sufficient and relevant textual evidence to support your response.
- Write an essay in which you explain how Emerson develops his claim about nonconformity and supports his argument. What is his main claim and how is it supported? Cite relevant evidence from the essay to develop your response (consider use of logos, pathos, ethos, and techniques).

Formative Assessment

1. Ask students to respond to the following prompt in a single paragraph: *How effective is Emerson in developing his argument about being a nonconformist? Support your answer by referring to elements of effective argumentation.*
2. Use the scoring guidelines in Figure 10.2 to evaluate students' assessments.

Effective Rhetoric	
0	Provides no response.
1	Response is limited and vague. Response only partially answers the question. A rhetorical element is not mentioned.
2	Response is accurate with 1–2 rhetorical elements named. Response includes limited or no evidence from text. Or response includes evidence from text, but does not relate to a rhetorical element.
3	Response is appropriate and accurate, describing 1–2 rhetorical elements to support effective argumentation. Response includes some evidence from the text.
4	Response is insightful and well supported, describing 2–3 rhetorical elements. Response includes evidence from the text.

Figure 10.2. Scoring guidelines for Lesson 10 formative assessment.

Handout 10.1
Excerpts from "Self-Reliance" *by Ralph Waldo Emerson*

I read the other day some verses written by an eminent painter which were original and not conventional. The soul always hears an admonition in such lines, let the subject be what it may. The sentiment they instil is of more value than any thought they may contain. To believe your own thought, to believe that what is true for you in your private heart is true for all men,—that is genius. Speak your latent conviction, and it shall be the universal sense; for the inmost in due time becomes the outmost,—and our first thought is rendered back to us by the trumpets of the Last Judgment. Familiar as the voice of the mind is to each, the highest merit we ascribe to Moses, Plato, and Milton is, that they set at naught books and traditions, and spoke not what men but what they thought. A man should learn to detect and watch that gleam of light which flashes across his mind from within, more than the lustre of the firmament of bards and sages. Yet he dismisses without notice his thought, because it is his. In every work of genius we recognize our own rejected thoughts: they come back to us with a certain alienated majesty. Great works of art have no more affecting lesson for us than this. They teach us to abide by our spontaneous impression with good-humored inflexibility then most when the whole cry of voices is on the other side. Else, to-morrow a stranger will say with masterly good sense precisely what we have thought and felt all the time, and we shall be forced to take with shame our own opinion from another.

There is a time in every man's education when he arrives at the conviction that envy is ignorance; that imitation is suicide; that he must take himself for better, for worse, as his portion; that though the wide universe is full of good, no kernel of nourishing corn can come to him but through his toil bestowed on that plot of ground which is given to him to till. The power which resides in him is new in nature, and none but he knows what that is which he can do, nor does he know until he has tried . . . .

. . . Trust thyself: every heart vibrates to that iron string. Accept the place the divine providence has found for you, the society of your contemporaries, the connection of events. Great men have always done so, and confided themselves childlike to the genius of their age, betraying their perception that the absolutely trustworthy was seated at their heart, working through their hands, predominating in all their being. And we are now men, and must accept in the highest mind the same transcendent destiny; and not minors and invalids in a protected corner, not cowards fleeing before a revolution, but guides, redeemers, and benefactors, obeying the Almighty effort, and advancing on Chaos and the Dark . . . .

. . . These are the voices which we hear in solitude, but they grow faint and inaudible as we enter into the world. Society everywhere is in conspiracy against the manhood of every one of its members. Society is a joint-stock company, in which the members agree, for the better securing of his bread to each shareholder, to surrender the liberty and culture of the eater. The virtue in most request is conformity. Self-reliance is its aversion. It loves not realities and creators, but names and customs.

Whoso would be a man must be a nonconformist. He who would gather immortal palms must not be hindered by the name of goodness, but must explore if it be goodness. Nothing is at last sacred but the integrity of your own mind . . . .

Handout 10.2
Selected Quote

_____

A foolish consistency is the hobgoblin of little minds, adored by little states-men and philosophers and divines. With consistency a great soul has sim-ply nothing to do. He may as well concern himself with his shadow on the wall. Speak what you think now in hard words, and to-morrow speak what to-morrow thinks in hard words again, though it contradict everything you said to-day.—"Ah, so you shall be sure to be misunderstood."—Is it so bad, then, to be misunderstood? Pythagoras was misunderstood, and Socrates, and Jesus, and Luther, and Copernicus, and Galileo, and Newton, and every pure and wise spirit that ever took flesh. To be great is to be misunderstood.

—Excerpt from "Self-Reliance" by Ralph Waldo Emerson

1. What is meant by the first sentence?

2. What is meant by "consistency?"

3. What evidence from the text makes you think this?

Handout 10.2, Continued

4. Paraphrase each sentence into a text message (you can include emojis).

5. What does this reveal about individuality versus conformity?

6. How does this relate to you?

Name: _____ Date: _____

Handout 10.3

Blank Rhetorical Analysis Wheel

Directions: Draw arrows across elements to show connections.

Text: _____

Purpose/Context

Point of View

Logos

Techniques

Pathos

Claim

Ethos

Structure/
Organization

Implications

Evaluation

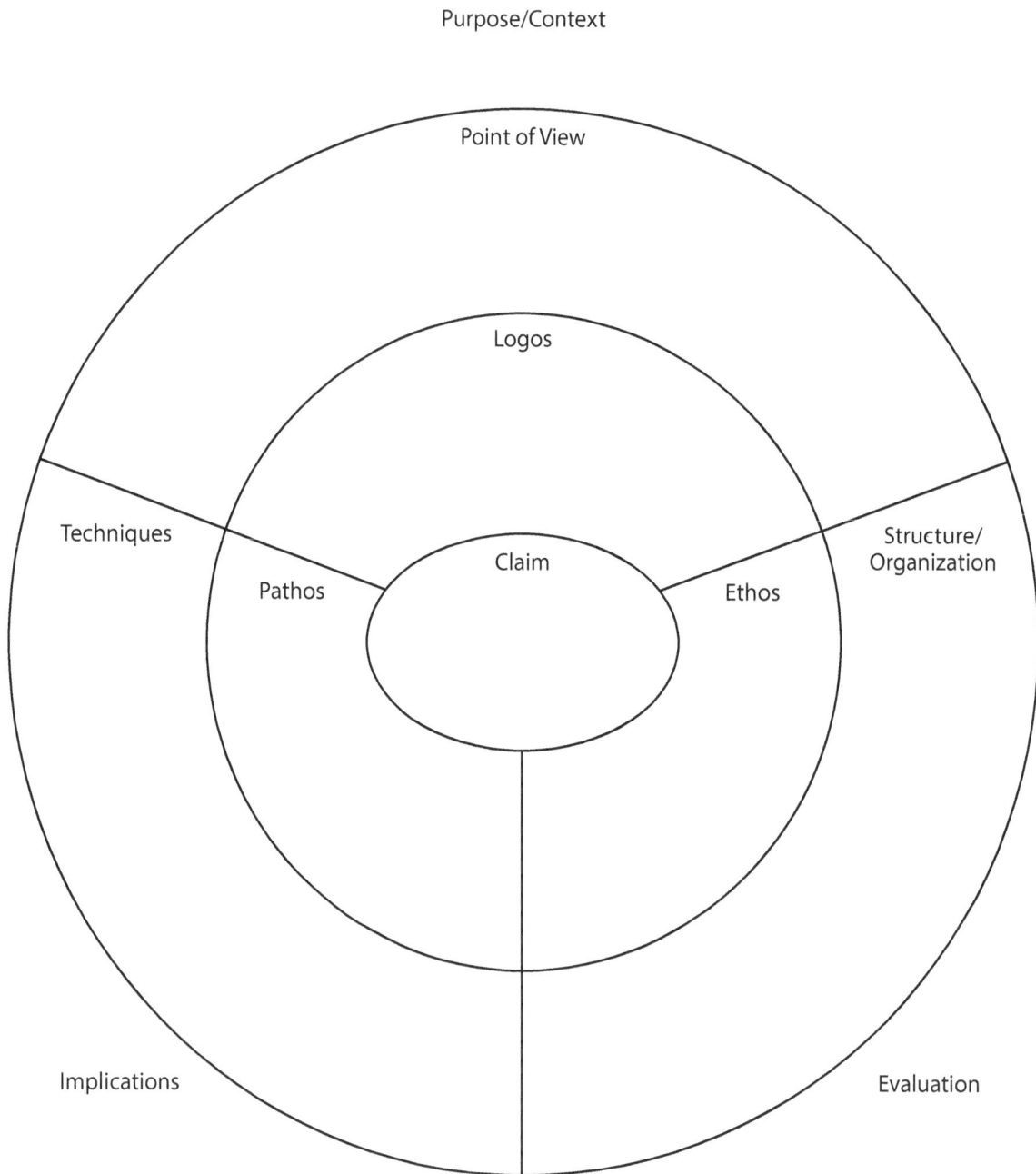

Created by Emily Mofield, Ed.D., & Tamra Stambaugh, Ph.D., 2015.

This page intentionally left blank.

Lesson

11

Excerpts From "Civil Disobedience"
by Henry David Thoreau

Goals/Objectives

Content: To analyze and interpret texts and art, students will be able to:
- explain with evidence how a writer supports a claim,
- respond to interpretations of texts through a variety of contexts by justifying ideas and providing new information,
- compare and contrast texts and real-world events on theme, and
- evaluate rhetoric within primary sources.

Process: To develop thinking, writing, and communication skills, students will be able to:
- use evidence to develop and support inferences,
- evaluate the use of effective argumentation, and
- analyze societal or individual conflicts resulting from the struggle between individuality versus conformity.

Concept: To understand the concept of individuality versus conformity in the language arts, students will be able to:
- support conformity versus individuality generalizations with evidence,
- develop and apply generalizations of additional key concepts, and
- explain the conflict between conformity and individuality.

Accelerated CCSS ELA Standards

RI.9-10.1	RI.9-10.9	RH.9-10.5
RI.9-10.2	SL.9-10.1	RH.9-10.6
RI.9-10.3	SL.9-10.1c	RH.9-10.8
RI.9-10.4	SL.9-10.1d	RH.9-10.9
RI.9-10.5	RH.9-10.1	W.9-10.4
RI.9-10.6	RH.9-10.2	
RI.9-10.7	RH.9-10.4	

 DOI: 10.4324/9781003235620-18

Materials

- (Optional) Student copies of Blank Rhetorical Analysis Wheel and/or Big Idea Reflection (see Appendix B)
- Student copies of previous lesson texts ("Harrison Bergeron" by Kurt Vonnegut [retrieved online] and excerpts from Emerson's "Self-Reliance" [Handout 10.1])
- Handout 11.1: Excerpts From "Civil Disobedience" by Henry David Thoreau
- Rubric 1: Product Rubric (Appendix C)

Introductory Activities

1. Ask students to think about an individual who has impacted change in society. This individual can be someone known worldwide, nationally, or locally. Once each student has selected someone, ask him or her to share with a partner who he or she selected and why. Then ask the following questions:
   - How was your person a change agent?
   - How was change accomplished?
   - What opposition did your individual face or create?

   Link student comments to issues of civil disobedience and explain how many individuals who made major changes (e.g., Rosa Parks) disobeyed societal rules they felt were unjust. Students will be looking at someone like that in this lesson as they study Henry David Thoreau.

2. **Engage students in a quick debate.** Ask: *Agree or disagree? Change cannot happen without conflict.* They may stand on opposite sides of the room based on their point of view to discuss.

3. Explain that Thoreau held strong feelings against slavery and the Mexican-American War and wrote about them in his essay "Civil Disobedience." He refused to pay poll taxes because of his views about slavery and the war. Students will read his reasoning in his essay. Ask students to conduct background information on Henry David Thoreau and present information to the class. Students may explore the following:
   - His childhood
   - People who influenced him
   - The movement of Transcendentalism
   - His views about current events during his time (e.g., slavery and the Mexican-American War)
   - His ideas on tax resistance
   - Reasons for imprisonment

- Information about his books/essays
- His influence on Gandhi and Martin Luther King Jr.

4. Present the term *civil disobedience.* Ask: *What do you think this means? Is this an oxymoron? In what context have you heard this term?* Tell students: *As you read the text, ask yourself, "Does civil disobedience mean being disobedient in a civil way, or to disobey civil society?"* Note: This title is often misunderstood by the general population. Thoreau is referring to disobeying civil society. Students may arrive at this conclusion after reading the text. As students read, encourage them think of how this text relates to both Emerson and "Harrison Bergeron" by Kurt Vonnegut.

Read Text

Distribute Handout 11.1: Excerpts From "Civil Disobedience" by Henry David Thoreau. Ask students to highlight quotes they think are important as it is read. Encourage students to read first independently, then read as a group, a paragraph at time.

Text-Dependent Questions

Select from the following text-dependent questions for a Socratic seminar or class discussion:

- What three choices does Thoreau give the reader regarding dealing with unjust laws?
- Why does Thoreau use so many questions in developing his argument? (Sample response: To elicit personal reflection.)
- What is meant by "the remedy is worse than the evil" and what solution does Thoreau offer?
- Thoreau uses the metaphor "machine of government" to develop his ideas. Using evidence from the text, why is this metaphor used?
- What solution does Thoreau offer to stop the machine?
- What specifically is Thoreau asking the abolitionists of Massachusetts to do and why does Thoreau offer this demand with urgency?
- According to Thoreau, what does the poll tax allow the state to accomplish? What are the two alternatives for the state to do if people refuse to pay a poll tax?
- What is Thoreau referring to when he asserts, "a minority is powerless when it conforms to the majority"?

- Thoreau explains his experience in jail for not paying a poll tax. Was this a positive or negative experience for him? Support your answer with sufficient evidence from the text.
- How does the last paragraph relate to individuality versus conformity?
- "If a plant cannot live according to its nature, it dies; and so a man." How does this metaphor relate to Thoreau's ideas about government and people?
- Now that you have read the text, how would Thoreau define civil disobedience? Is it disobeying authority in a civil way or disobeying civil society? Use the text to defend your answer. (*Note:* Thoreau defines civil disobedience as disobeying civil society.)

In-Class Activities to Deepen Learning

1. Have students make comparisons of how Harrison Bergeron puts into action the ideas of Thoreau and/or Emerson. Students may refer to texts from previous lessons. Students should cite specific quotes from both texts they compare and complete a Venn diagram or comparison chart.
2. Discuss the following quotes from Socrates and John F. Kennedy. Socrates: "An individual must do what his city or country demands of him or he must change their view of what is just." Kennedy: "Ask not what your country can do for you but what you can do for your country." Have students develop a skit that shows how Thoreau's thoughts contrast with Socrates and John F. Kennedy. How would Thoreau respond to these ideas? Develop a mini skit or three-way conversation among the individuals to show your understanding.
3. Have students complete a Big Idea Reflection on Thoreau's ideas (see Appendix B).
4. Have students complete a Blank Rhetorical Analysis Wheel (see Appendix B) on Thoreau's speech. Consider the following:
   - **Context:** Consider his historical stance against slavery (point of view and assumptions) and that taxes support a government, which supports slavery.
   - **Claim:** The government is corrupt in supporting slavery, thus the government should not be supported.
   - **Logos:** He develops several points including (1) the government is a machine that must be stopped with individuals' friction, (2) abolitionists should withdraw their support for the government, (3) do not pay poll taxes to support the government, (4) his experience in prison justified the foolishness of a state's institutions, and (5) the government cannot affect a strong mind, only the body. He uses rhetorical questions (first paragraph), metaphors (government machine, trees, nuts, plants), and religious appeals (God on our side) as techniques to support these points.

- **Ethos:** Thoreau brings credibility to his argument by explaining he himself has been in prison and disobeyed "civil" society by not paying his taxes.
- **Pathos:** His series of rhetorical questions at the beginning build a sense of urgency to the audience. He appeals to moral obligations throughout the text. Consider how his bias affects his emotional appeals. Where are emotional appeals the strongest?

5. Conduct an improv talk show with a host and the following characters as guests:
   - A Separatist from the *Mayflower*
   - Maya Angelou
   - Emily Dickinson
   - Pablo Picasso
   - Mr. Bittering (from "Dark They Were and Golden-Eyed")
   - Margot (from "All Summer in a Day")
   - Harrison Bergeron
   - Henry David Thoreau
   - Ralph Waldo Emerson
   - Eleanor Roosevelt
   - Members of the audience (ideally, every student should have a part)

Assign roles and give students 5 minutes for silent thinking time. Help students prepare by asking each participant to plan for the talk show:
- **Guest characters:** Jot down ideas for answers to the questions they will be asked: *Did you choose to conform to the group or to act on individuality? What was this experience like? What consequences did you face? Do you have any regrets or advice? Which other guest do you share most similar experiences with?*
- **Audience members:** Jot down unanswered questions from previous lessons for a particular guest. Questions should relate to lesson concepts and ideally to the theme of individuality versus conformity.
- **Host:** Prepare order of questions and flow of show (15–20 min. show). The host should lead in a discussion such as the following: *Guests are here today to discuss their experiences with conformity versus individuality. Each guest has experienced the struggle in some significant way. Did you choose to conform to the group or to act on individuality? What was this experience like? What consequences did you face? Do you have any regrets or advice? With which other guest do you share the most similar experiences?* The host should also call on audience members to ask their unanswered questions.

Additionally, the host could ask some key questions (from VanTassel-Baska, 1988) that have been addressed throughout the unit:

- Is conformity good or bad?
- Is it natural for an individual to want to contribute to his society?
- What must humans do to insure the survival of their society?
- What conflicts does an individual face as a member of society? How important is conformity?

Concept Connections

Discuss connections to individuality versus conformity by asking the following question: *How does Thoreau show the cyclic nature of individuality and conformity—individuality leads to conformity and vice versa?* Students may reflect on concept connections using Handout 1.3: Concept Organizer, continued from previous lessons. Figure 11.1 provides some sample responses.

Choice-Based Differentiated Products

Students may choose one of the following independent products to complete (*Note*: Use Rubric 1: Product Rubric in Appendix C to assess student products):

- Develop a skit that shows interaction between Emerson, Thoreau, and the character of Harrison Bergeron, meeting during the present year. They should discuss how their ideas are similar and different and how they see each of their ideas in contemporary life.
- Read and apply a rhetorical analysis (using the Rhetorical Analysis Wheel) to Martin Luther King Jr.'s "Letter From Birmingham Jail." In an essay or multimedia presentation, explain how King applies Thoreau's ideas. Cite specific evidence from both the letter and Thoreau's excerpt.
- Thoreau's ideas were not always accepted; some claim his ideas promote anarchy. Write an editorial that presents your opinion about Thoreau's ideas. If he were to present his ideas today, how would this affect America? Refer to the conflict of the individual versus society within your editorial.
- Research Thoreau's influence on Mahatma Gandhi. In a multimedia presentation or essay, explain how Gandhi's ideas and actions relate to Thoreau's text. Include at least three quotes from Thoreau's texts and three sources relating to Gandhi in your product.
- Create a song that reflects Thoreau's ideas about civil disobedience. Include at least four of Thoreau's points within your song and perform it for the class.

Both conformity and individuality are agents of change.
If everyone conformed to abolitionist thinking, then the government would have to end slavery. Thoreau asserts that individuals should conform to the abolitionist cause and slavery should end.
Both conformity and individuality involve sacrifice.
Being an individual against the government majority (conformity) may involve punishment.
There are positives and negatives to both conformity and individuality.
Being an individual against conforming to Massachusetts's government by not paying the poll tax results in incarceration, but if everyone did this, then the government would have to agree to end slavery.
Examine the relationship between conformity, individuality, and another related concept.
Students may examine the relationship between majority, minority, power, freedom, and influence.

Figure 11.1. *How does Thoreau show the cyclic nature of individuality and conformity—individuality leads to conformity and vice versa?* Sample responses.

ELA Practice Tasks

Assign one of the following tasks as a performance-based assessment for this lesson:

- Does Thoreau believe the individual or society is a more powerful force? In a multiparagraph essay, develop an argument that cites sufficient and relevant evidence from Thoreau's text to support your claim.
- Compare and contrast both Emerson and Thoreau's approaches in developing ideas about nonconformity. How do they approach the topic differently? What generalizations can be made about both works? In an essay, refer to specific textual evidence in excerpts from both "Self-Reliance" and "Civil Disobedience" to support your response.

Formative Assessment

1. Ask students to respond to the following prompt in a single paragraph: *How effective is Thoreau in developing his argument to not pay taxes? Support your answer by referring to elements of effective argumentation.*
2. Use the scoring guidelines in Figure 11.2 to evaluate students' assessments.

	Effective Rhetoric
0	Provides no response.
1	Response is limited and vague. Response only partially answers the question. A rhetorical element is not mentioned.
2	Response is accurate with 1–2 rhetorical elements named. Response includes limited or no evidence from text. Or response includes evidence from text, but does not relate to a rhetorical element.
3	Response is appropriate and accurate, describing 1–2 rhetorical elements to support effective argumentation. Response includes some evidence from the text.
4	Response is insightful and well supported, describing 2–3 rhetorical elements. Response includes evidence from the text.

Figure 11.2. Scoring guidelines for Lesson 11 formative assessment.

Handout 11.1

Excerpts From "Civil Disobedience" *by Henry David Thoreau*

Unjust laws exist: shall we be content to obey them, or shall we endeavor to amend them, and obey them until we have succeeded, or shall we transgress them at once? Men, generally, under such a government as this, think that they ought to wait until they have persuaded the majority to alter them. They think that, if they should resist, the remedy would be worse than the evil. But it is the fault of the government itself that the remedy is worse than the evil. It makes it worse. Why is it not more apt to anticipate and provide for reform? Why does it not cherish its wise minority? Why does it cry and resist before it is hurt? Why does it not encourage its citizens to put out its faults, and do better than it would have them? Why does it always crucify Christ and excommunicate Copernicus and Luther, and pronounce Washington and Franklin rebels . . . ?

. . . If the injustice is part of the necessary friction of the machine of government, let it go, let it go: perchance it will wear smooth—certainly the machine will wear out. If the injustice has a spring, or a pulley, or a rope, or a crank, exclusively for itself, then perhaps you may consider whether the remedy will not be worse than the evil; but if it is of such a nature that it requires you to be the agent of injustice to another, then I say, break the law. Let your life be a counter-friction to stop the machine. What I have to do is to see, at any rate, that I do not lend myself to the wrong which I condemn.

As for adopting the ways which the State has provided for remedying the evil, I know not of such ways. They take too much time, and a man's life will be gone. I have other affairs to attend to. I came into this world, not chiefly to make this a good place to live in, but to live in it, be it good or bad. A man has not everything to do, but something; and because he cannot do everything, it is not necessary that he should be doing something wrong. It is not my business to be petitioning the Governor or the Legislature any more than it is theirs to petition me; and if they should not hear my petition, what should I do then? But in this case the State has provided no way: its very Constitution is the evil. This may seem to be harsh and stubborn and unconcilliatory; but it is to treat with the utmost kindness and consideration the only spirit that can appreciate or deserves it. So is all change for the better, like birth and death, which convulse the body.

I do not hesitate to say, that those who call themselves Abolitionists should at once effectually withdraw their support, both in person and property, from the government of Massachusetts, and not wait till they constitute a majority of one, before they suffer the right to prevail through them. I think that it is enough if they have God on their side, without waiting for that other one. Moreover, any man more right than his neighbors constitutes a majority of one already.

I meet this American government, or its representative, the State government, directly, and face to face, once a year—no more—in the person of its tax-gatherer; this is the only mode in which a man situated as I am necessarily meets it; and it then says distinctly, Recognize me; and the simplest, the most effectual, and, in the present posture of affairs, the indispensablest mode of treating with it on this head, of expressing your little satisfaction with and love for it, is to deny it then. My civil neighbor, the tax-gatherer, is the very man I have to deal with—for it is, after all, with men and not with parchment that I quarrel—and he has voluntarily chosen to be an agent of the government. How shall he ever know well that he is and does as an officer of the government, or as a man, until he is obliged to consider whether he will treat me, his neighbor, for whom he has respect, as a neighbor and well-disposed man, or as a maniac and disturber of the peace, and see if he can get over this obstruction to his neighborlines without a ruder and more impetuous thought or speech corresponding with his action. I know this well, that if one thousand, if one hundred, if ten men whom I could name—if ten honest men only—ay, if one HONEST man, in this State of Massachusetts, ceasing to hold slaves, were actually to withdraw from this co-partnership, and be locked up in the county jail therefor, it would be the abolition of slavery in America. For it matters not how small the beginning may seem to be: what is once well done is done forever. But we love better to talk about it: that we say is our mission. Reform keeps many scores of newspapers in its service, but not one man. If my esteemed neighbor, the State's ambassador, who will devote his days to the settlement of the question of human rights in the Council Chamber, instead of being threatened with the prisons of Carolina, were to sit down the prisoner of Massachusetts, that State which is so anxious to foist the sin of slavery upon her sister—though at present she can discover only an act of inhospitality to be the ground of a quarrel with her—the Legislature would not wholly waive the subject of the following winter.

Under a government which imprisons unjustly, the true place for a just man is also a prison. The proper place today, the only place which Massachusetts has provided for her freer and less despondent spirits, is in her prisons, to be put out and locked out of the State by her own act, as they have already put themselves out by their principles. It is there that the fugitive slave, and the Mexican prisoner on parole, and the Indian come to plead the wrongs of his race should find them; on that separate but more free and honorable ground, where the State places those who are not with her, but against her—the only house in a slave State in which a free man can abide with honor. If any think that their influence would be lost there, and their voices no longer afflict the ear of the State, that they would not be as an enemy within its walls, they do not know by how much truth is stronger than error, nor how much more eloquently and effectively he can combat injustice who has experienced a little in his own person. Cast your whole vote, not a strip of paper merely, but your whole influence. A minority is powerless while it conforms to the majority; it is not even a minority then; but it is irresistible when it clogs by its whole weight. If the alternative is to keep all just men in prison, or give up war and slavery, the State will not hesitate which to choose. If a thousand men were not to pay their tax bills this year, that would not be a violent and bloody measure, as it would be to pay them, and enable the State to commit violence and shed innocent blood. This is, in fact, the definition of a peaceable revolution, if any such is possible. If the tax-gatherer, or any other public officer, asks me, as one has done, "But what shall I do?" my answer is, "If you really wish to do anything, resign your office." When the subject has refused allegiance, and the officer has resigned from office, then the revolution is accomplished. But even suppose blood should flow. Is there not a sort of blood shed when the conscience is wounded? Through this wound a man's real manhood and immortality flow out, and he bleeds to an everlasting death. I see this blood flowing now . . .

. . . I have paid no poll tax for six years. I was put into a jail once on this account, for one night; and, as I stood considering the walls of solid stone, two or three feet thick, the door of wood and iron, a foot thick, and the iron grating which strained the light, I could not help being struck with the foolishness of that institution which treated me as if I were mere flesh and blood and bones, to be locked up. I wondered that it should have concluded at length that this was the best use it could put me to, and had never thought to avail itself of my services in some way. I saw that, if there was a wall of stone between me and my townsmen, there was a still more difficult one to climb or break through before they could get to be as free as I was. I did not for a moment feel confined, and the walls seemed a great waste of stone and mortar. I felt as if I alone of all my townsmen had paid my tax. They plainly did not know how to treat me, but behaved like persons who are underbred. In every threat and in every compliment there was a blunder; for they thought that my chief desire was to stand the other side of that stone wall. I could not but smile to see how industriously they locked the door on my meditations, which followed them out again without let or hindrance, and they were really all that was dangerous. As they could not reach me, they had resolved to punish my body; just as boys, if they cannot come at some person against whom they have a spite, will abuse his dog. I saw that the State was half-witted, that it was timid as a lone woman with her silver spoons, and that it did not know its friends from its foes, and I lost all my remaining respect for it, and pitied it.

Thus the state never intentionally confronts a man's sense, intellectual or moral, but only his body, his senses. It is not armed with superior wit or honesty, but with superior physical strength. I was not born to be forced. I will breathe after my own fashion. Let us see who is the strongest. What force has a multitude? They only can force me who obey a higher law than I. They force me to become like themselves. I do not hear of men being forced to live this way or that by masses of men. What sort of life were that to live? When I meet a government which says to me, "Your money or your life," why should I be in haste to give it my money? It may be in a great strait, and not know what to do: I cannot help that. It must help itself; do as I do. It is not worth the while to snivel about it. I am not responsible for the successful working of the machinery of society. I am not the son of the engineer. I perceive that, when an acorn and a chestnut fall side by side, the one does not remain inert to make way for the other, but both obey their own laws, and spring and grow and flourish as best they can, till one, perchance, overshadows and destroys the other. If a plant cannot live according to nature, it dies; and so a man . . .

Lesson

12

Final Reflection and Culminating Project

Goals/Objectives

Content: To analyze and interpret texts and art, students will be able to:
- explain with evidence how literary and/or visual elements contribute to the overall meaning of a work,
- explain with evidence how a writer supports a claim,
- respond to interpretations of texts through a variety of contexts by justifying ideas and providing new information,
- compare and contrast texts and real-world events on theme, and
- evaluate rhetoric within primary sources.

Process: To develop thinking, writing, and communication skills, students will be able to:
- reason through an issue by analyzing points of view, assumptions, and implications;
- use evidence to develop and support inferences;
- evaluate the use of effective argumentation; and
- analyze societal or individual conflicts resulting from the struggle between individuality versus conformity.

Concept: To understand the concept of individuality versus conformity in the language arts, students will be able to:
- support conformity versus individuality generalizations with evidence,
- develop and apply generalizations of additional key concepts, and
- explain the conflict between conformity and individuality.

Materials

- Handout 12.1: *I, Me, You, We* Culminating Project
- Students may need copies of the Blank Literary Analysis Wheel, Big Idea Reflection, Blank Rhetorical Analysis Wheel, Blank Visual Analysis Wheel,

 DOI: 10.4324/9781003235620-19

Reasoning About a Situation or Event, and/or Handout 1.3: Concept Organizer, depending on the project they choose (see Appendix B for models)

- Rubric 3: Culminating Project Rubric (Appendix C)

Discussion

1. Remind students about the concepts explored in this unit.
   - Both conformity and individuality are agents of change.
   - Both conformity and individuality involve sacrifice.
   - There are positives and negatives to both conformity and individuality.

2. Students should review their responses on concept organizers from previous lessons. Ask: *What patterns do you notice? Do you see any similarities? What are the major contrasts? What other generalizations about individuality versus conformity can you make based on this unit? What evidence is there to support those generalizations?*

Student Independent Reflection

Assign the student reflections on Handout 12.1: *I, Me, You, We* Culminating Project (you may choose to assign all of them or part of them).

Choice-Based Differentiated Products

Assign the culminating project (see Handout 12.1). At teacher discretion, students can present parts of their projects to the class. Use Rubric 3: Culminating Project Rubric to assess student products and applied learning.

Culminating ELA Practice Task

Assign the following task as a culminating performance-based assessment: *After reading several texts about conformity versus individuality, what conclusions can you draw concerning the role of the individual within a group (society)? Argue whether an individual or society is a more powerful agent of change. Refer to at least four texts from the unit, citing textual evidence from these texts to support your claim.*

Handout 12.1

I, Me, You, We Culminating Project

STUDENT REFLECTION

Directions: What other movies, stories, art, historical events, or current events involve the following generalizations in *I, Me, You, We*? Explain how one story or event demonstrates each concept.

1. Text/Event: _____
   Both conformity and individuality are agents of change.

2. Text/Event: _____
   Both conformity and individuality involve sacrifice.

3. Text/Event: _____
   There are positives and negatives to both conformity and individuality.

4. Write a personal reflection regarding the following questions. How does the theme of individuality versus conformity relate to your own life? You may consider your own identity. Does where you are change who you are? Are there times you challenge the status quo? Are there times you mask your true identity to conform to a group? What new insight do you have about these concepts as a result of this unit?

CULMINATING PROJECT

Directions: Choose one activity to demonstrate your understanding of the content, processes, and concepts presented in this unit:

1. Create your own short story that uses the individuality versus conformity theme. Complete a Literary Analysis Wheel for your own story. Also provide concept support by completing Handout 1.3: Concept Organizer for the theme of individuality versus conformity. Include development of dialogue, point of view, setting, plot elements, characterization, symbols, and theme within your story.
2. Study three pieces of visual art that you think relate to the theme of individuality versus conformity in some way. Complete a Visual Analysis Wheel on each piece. Then, create a three-way Venn diagram on the pieces. Explain in a paragraph or two how each piece exemplifies the theme of individuality versus conformity. Show the pieces of art to the class and explain the themes to your classmates.
3. Find a primary source that relates to the lives of two individuals introduced in this unit: Ray Bradbury, William Bradford, Pablo Picasso, Eleanor Roosevelt, Ralph Waldo Emerson, Henry David Thoreau, Maya Angelou, Emily Dickinson, etc. (letters, diaries, autobiographies, interviews, essays they have written). Biographies or information written about them on the Internet are not primary sources. In what ways is the individuality versus conformity theme evidenced in each of their life experiences and/or works? Explain in a couple of paragraphs and include a list of your sources.
4. Use Reasoning About a Situation or Event to think through the following issue—Which should be most highly valued, the individual or society?—as the situation. Choose four individuals from the unit (characters or real people). Then, create a visual collage or multimedia movie to answer the question "Which should be most highly valued, the individual or society?" Incorporate abstract symbols, words, pic-

tures, and quotes about individuality, identity, conformity, society, belongingness, etc. Also turn in a written description of symbols used. See Rubric 2: Collage Rubric.

5. Consider real-life applications of the lessons presented (e.g., affirmative action, teens masking their true identity to fit into a group, school uniforms, bullying, global civil rights, minority versus majority, unjust rules within societies). Develop a community service project related to addressing a problem surfaced within this unit. Complete Reasoning About a Situation or Event concerning the stakeholders involved in the issue. Develop a proposal and get it approved by your teacher. Consider working with your community/school to implement the action plan.

Culminating ELA Practice Task

After reading several texts about conformity versus individuality, what conclusions can you draw concerning the role of the individual within a group (society)? Argue whether an individual or society is a more powerful agent of change. Refer to at least four texts from the unit, citing textual evidence from these texts to support your claim.

Name: _____ Date: _____

Posttest
"The Man, The Boy, and the Donkey" *by Aesop*

Directions: Read the text and write your responses to the questions below citing evidence from the text. After reading, complete the questions within 30 minutes.

A Man and his son were once going with their Donkey to market. As they were walking along by its side a countryman passed them and said: "You fools, what is a Donkey for but to ride upon?"

So the Man put the Boy on the Donkey and they went on their way. But soon they passed a group of men, one of whom said: "See that lazy youngster, he lets his father walk while he rides."

So the Man ordered his Boy to get off, and got on himself. But they hadn't gone far when they passed two women, one of whom said to the other: "Shame on that lazy lout to let his poor little son trudge along."

Well, the Man didn't know what to do, but at last he took his Boy up before him on the Donkey. By this time they had come to the town, and the passers-by began to jeer and point at them. The Man stopped and asked what they were scoffing at. The men said: "Aren't you ashamed of yourself for overloading that poor Donkey of yours—you and your hulking son?"

The Man and Boy got off and tried to think what to do. They thought and they thought, till at last they cut down a pole, tied the Donkey's feet to it, and raised the pole and the Donkey to their shoulders. They went along amid the laughter of all who met them till they came to Market Bridge, when the Donkey, getting one of his feet loose, kicked out and caused the Boy to drop his end of the pole. In the struggle the Donkey fell over the bridge, and his fore-feet being tied together he was drowned.

"That will teach you," said an old man who had followed them.

QUESTIONS

1. How does the author's use of literary techniques (e.g., point of view, conflict, plot, language, symbolism, characterization, setting, etc.) contribute to the overall meaning of the passage?

2. "They thought and thought, till at last they cut down a pole, tied the Donkey's feet to it, and raised the pole and the Donkey to their shoulders." What inferences can be made about the man's motivation and conflict?

3. What does this story suggest about individuality versus conformity?

Name: _____   Date: _____

Posttest Rubric
"The Man, The Boy, and the Donkey" *by Aesop*

	0	1	2	3	4
Question 1: Content: Literary Analysis	Provides no response.	Response is limited and vague. There is no connection to how literary elements contribute to the meaning, main idea, or theme. A literary element is merely named.	Response is accurate, with 1–2 literary techniques described with vague or no connection to a main idea or theme. Response includes limited or no evidence from text.	Response is appropriate and accurate, describing at least 2 literary elements and a main idea or theme. Response is literal and includes some evidence from the text.	Response is insightful and well supported, describing at least 2 literary elements and the theme. Response includes abstract connections and substantial evidence from the text.
Question 2: Inference From Evidence	Provides no response.	Response is limited, vague, and/or inaccurate. There is no justification for answers given.	Response is accurate, but lacks adequate explanation. Response includes some justification for either the character's motivation or conflict.	Response is accurate and makes sense. Response includes some justification about the character's motivation and conflict.	Response is accurate, insightful, interpretive, and well written. Response includes thoughtful justification about the character's motivation and conflict.
Question 3: Concept/Theme	Provides no response.	Response is limited, vague, and/or inaccurate.	Response lacks adequate explanation. Response does not relate or create a generalization about individuality versus conformity. Little or no evidence from text.	Response is accurate and makes sense. Response relates to or creates an idea about individuality versus conformity with some relation to the text.	Response is accurate, insightful, and well written. Response relates to or creates a generalization about individuality versus conformity with evidence from the text.

Note: Adapted from *Jacob's Ladder Reading Comprehension Program: Level 4* (p. 148) by T. Stambaugh & J. VanTassel-Baska, 2001, New York, NY: Taylor & Francis. Copyright 2001 by Taylor & Francis. Adapted with permission.

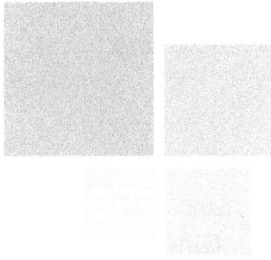

References

Assouline, S., Colangelo, N., VanTassel-Baska, J., & Lupkowski-Shoplik, A. (2015). (Eds). *A nation empowered: Evidence trumps the excuses holding back America's brightest students*. Iowa City: University of Iowa, The Connie Belin & Jacqueline N. Blank International Center for Gifted Education and Talent Development.

Center for Gifted Education. (n.d.). Reasoning about a situation or event. *Teaching Models*. Retrieved from http://education.wm.edu/centers/cfge/curriculum/teachingmodels

Colangelo, N., Assouline, S., & Gross, M.U.M. (2004). *A nation deceived: How schools hold back America's brightest students* (Vol. II.). Iowa City: University of Iowa, The Connie Belin & Jacqueline N. Blank International Center for Gifted Education and Talent Development.

Cromar, W. (n.d.). Art 314 - Geometry. *New Media Abington*. Retrieved from http://newmediaabington.pbworks.com/w/page/28779892/ART%20314%20-%20Geometry

Kulik, J. A., & Kulik, C.-L. C. (1992). Meta-analytic findings on grouping programs. *Gifted Child Quarterly, 36*, 73–77.

Morris, S. B., & DeShon, R. P. (2002). Combining effect size estimates in meta-analysis with repeated measures and independent-groups designs. *Psychological Methods, 7*, 105–125.

Rogers, K. B. (2007). Lessons learned about educating the gifted and talented: A synthesis of the research on educational practice. *Gifted Child Quarterly, 51*, 382–396.

Shmoop Editorial Team. (2008). Alone Summary. *Shmoop*. Retrieved from http://www.shmoop.com/alone-angelou/summary.html

Stambaugh, T., & VanTassel-Baska, J. (2001). *Jacob's ladder reading comprehension program: Level 4*. Waco, TX: Prufrock Press.

Steenberger-Hu, S., & Moon, S. M. (2011). The effects of acceleration on high-ability learners: A meta-analysis. *Gifted Child Quarterly, 55*, 39–53.

VanTassel-Baska, J. (1986). Effective curriculum and instruction models for talented students. *Gifted Child Quarterly, 30*, 164–169.

VanTassel-Baska, J. (1988). The study of humanities. In J. VanTassel-Baska (Ed.), *Comprehensive curriculum of gifted learners* (pp. 274–275). Boston, MA: Allyn & Bacon.

160
VanTassel-Baska, J., & Stambaugh, T. (2008). *What works: 20 years of curriculum research and development for high-ability learners.* Center for Gifted Education, College of William and Mary. Waco, TX: Prufrock Press.

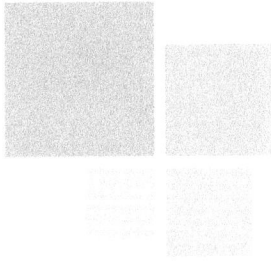

Appendix A
Instructions for Using the Models

LITERARY ANALYSIS WHEEL INSTRUCTIONS

The Literary Analysis Model is used to guide students through analyzing how an author uses literary techniques to develop meaning within a work. The model allows students to see connections between multiple literary elements (e.g., setting impacts conflict, conflict reveals character motives and values, characterization impacts theme, etc.).

Using the Literary Analysis Wheel

The Literary Analysis Wheel can be used to guide students through an analysis of a short story, poem, or novel. First, guide students to identify elements of the wheel separately, then emphasize a deeper analysis by asking how elements relate to each other (e.g., point of view impacts theme, setting creates mood, etc.).

The Literary Analysis Wheel is meant to be interactive. The inner wheel conceptually spins so that its elements interact with each other and the outer wheel. Each element can relate to each other, regardless of its placement on the wheel.

The Literary Analysis Wheel Guide (Appendix B) shows specific prompts for each element of the wheel. The teacher may simply refer to the model during instruction or students may take notes on the Blank Literary Analysis Wheel using arrows to show how the various elements relate. It is suggested that students note the answers to the "simple" questions on the graphic organizer, and then discuss interactions with other elements. Consider making a poster of the Literary Analysis Wheel Guide and posting it in your classroom for students to refer to throughout the unit.

Once students are accustomed to using the wheel, encourage students to develop their own questions about the relationship between elements.

Students can make their own interactive paper-plate model of the wheel. Two different colored papers may be used for the inner and outer circles, secured with a brass paper fastener. Students may use the wheels as visuals in small groups.

Sample questions for literary analysis. The following questions can be asked to support students in analyzing literature. Note that complexity is added by combining elements.

Simple:

- **Character:** *What are the values and motives of the characters? What evidence supports this? How does the author reveal character?*
- **Setting:** *What is the time and place of the story?*
- **Tone:** *What is the author's attitude toward the subject? With what attitude does the author approach the theme?*
- **Symbols:** *How do objects or names represent more abstract ideas?*
- **Point of View:** *What is the narrator's point of view (first person, third person objective, third person limited, third person omniscient)?*
- **Language/Style/Structure:** *What figurative language and imagery does the author use? What is the author's style?*
- **Plot/Conflict:** *What are the significant internal and external conflicts of the story? What are the significant parts of the plot?*
- **Mood:** *What is the feeling the reader gets from the story? How is this established?*
- **Theme:** *What is the author's main message that can be generalized to broader contexts? (The theme is the author's point of view on a given subject.)*

Complex:

- Setting+
  - *How does the setting influence the development of the theme?*
  - *How does the setting affect the mood?*
  - *What language does the author use to describe the setting (e.g., use of imagery, similes, etc.)?*
  - *How does the setting enhance conflict? How does the setting provoke plot events?*
  - *How is the setting symbolic of a larger idea (e.g., autumn, twilight)?*
  - *How does the setting affect and change the characters?*
  - *How does the setting help reveal the author's tone/attitude toward the theme/subject?*
  - *What conflicts could only happen in this setting? How does this influence the plot and theme?*

- Symbols+
  - *How do symbols help develop the theme?*
  - *How does the author use figurative language to establish symbolism?*
  - *How do symbols relate to key plot elements and conflicts?*

- ◆ *How do symbols contribute to establishing the mood?*
- ◆ *Is the setting symbolic of a larger idea (e.g., twilight, autumn)?*
- ◆ *How does the author's use of symbols reveal the author's tone?*
- ◆ *How are characters symbolic of archetypes? What symbols are associated with the characters?*

- Character+
  - ◆ *How do the characters' actions/beliefs/attitudes/struggles influence the theme?*
  - ◆ *How do the qualities of the characters affect the conflict as it relates to significant parts of the plot?*
  - ◆ *How do the characters' actions and responses establish mood?*
  - ◆ *What characters' thoughts/feelings are hidden and/or revealed by the narrator's point of view? How does this impact the reader's experience of the story?*
  - ◆ *How does the author use language to develop character? Consider dialect, descriptions, use of figurative language, and names.*
  - ◆ *Are characters revealed by symbols?*
  - ◆ *How does the setting affect character actions?*
  - ◆ *How does the author's tone toward the subject influence the development of characters?*

- Tone+
  - ◆ *How does the author's tone help establish the theme? What attitude does the author take in approaching the theme?*
  - ◆ *How is the author's tone revealed in the narrator's point of view (e.g. the narrator's words and feelings will reveal the attitude of how the author approaches the theme)?*
  - ◆ *What words/phrases does the author use to establish tone? How does the tone change throughout the story? How is this established through the author's style?*
  - ◆ *How is the author's tone revealed in the plot and conflicts? What specific textual evidence supports this?*
  - ◆ *How do the characters' conflicts reveal the author's tone toward a subject?*
  - ◆ *How does the author's tone aid in developing the mood of the story?*
  - ◆ *How do symbols help reveal the author's tone?*
  - ◆ *How do character actions, values, and conflicts reveal the author's tone?*
  - ◆ *How does the setting help reveal the author's tone/attitude toward the subject?*

- Point of View+
  - *How does the narrator's point of view shape the theme?*
  - *How does the narrator's point of view establish mood (e.g., the reader depends on the narrator's perspective in telling the story, so the reader feels the way the narrator does about what is being described)?*
  - *How does the narrator's point of view affect the way the reader views the significant conflicts and plot events?*
  - *What is the style of the narrator? How does the narrator's point of view (specifically, voice and diction) affect the story?*
  - *How is the author's tone revealed in the narrator's point of view (e.g. the narrator's words and feelings will reveal the attitude of how the author approaches the theme)?*
  - *What character thoughts are revealed or hidden because of the narrator's point of view? How does this impact the reader's experience of the story?*

- Language/Style/Structure+
  - *How does the author's use of figurative language or imagery contribute to literary elements?*
  - *How does the dialect of the characters contribute to our understanding of literary elements?*
  - *How does the author's style and sentence structure enhance the mood?*

- Mood+
  - *How does the mood help develop the theme? What if the mood were different, how would this change the theme of the story?*
  - *How does the author's point of view help create mood?*
  - *How does the author's tone create mood for the reader?*
  - *How do the character's actions, thoughts, and conflicts contribute to the mood?*
  - *How does the setting contribute to the mood?*
  - *How does the author use specific language to develop the mood?*
  - *How do specific symbols help establish the mood?*

- Plot/Conflict+
  - *How does the plot develop the theme? How would the theme be different if the story had a different ending?*
  - *How does the conflict reveal the character's values and motives?*
  - *How does setting impact the conflict and plot?*

> ◆ *What insight about the conflict does the reader have (or not have) as a result of the narrator's point of view?*
> ◆ *How do symbols represent aspects of the conflict (also consider foreshadowing devices)?*
> ◆ *How do character actions, thoughts, and conflicts reveal the author's tone?*
> ◆ *How does the plot and conflict reveal and/or change the mood?*
> ◆ *How does the author's style contribute to the development of the plot? Why does the author use more language/description on certain aspects of the plot than others?*

- Theme+
  - ◆ *How does the plot impact the theme? How would the theme change if key parts of the plot or ending were changed?*
  - ◆ *How does the theme impact the development of the plot? If the author wanted to show a different theme, how would he have to change the plot of the story? How would the characters' values, motives, and actions change?*
  - ◆ *How do the literary elements contribute to the development of the theme?*

- **Interpretation:**
  - *Taken altogether, what is your interpretation of the work (e.g., what is the explanation or meaning of this work given the author's use of various literary elements)? How did literary elements combine to create meaning? Support your interpretation by referring to the interaction of multiple elements in shaping your understanding of the work.*

Example Literary Analysis Lesson

Read the poem "I like to see it lap the Miles" by Emily Dickinson, available at http://www.poets.org/poetsorg/poem/i-see-it-lap-miles-43.

Step 1: Text-dependent questions. Lead students through a close reading of text. (*Note:* Do not give away that the poem is about a train; students should continue to hypothesize and discuss with textual evidence).

- According to the poem, does the author enjoy watching this object? How do you know? (Sample response: Yes, the first line of the poem states, "I like to see it . . . ")
- According to the poem, does the author like the object itself? How do you know? (Sample response: No, negative connotations about the object—supercilious, complaining, horrid, hooting—are combined with its omnip-

otence. It carves out the quarry to fit its own needs, to "fit its sides"—which is not welcomed in Dickinson's world.)

- What feelings can we associate with some of the words in this poem (horrid, hooting, omnipotent, supercilious, complaining, docile, punctual)? Are the connotations positive or negative?
- How do these connotations change and what effect does it have on the poem? (Sample response: They change from negative to positive.)
- After a second reading, students should respond to a partner: What is this poem about? (Most may say a horse, but help students understand that it is being compared to a horse, continue to guide them as they "discover" it is a railway train.) What evidence is there to support your idea? (The poem is about a train that is compared to a horse. Ask students to highlight or underline all comparisons of the train symbolized through a horse. Note that a train was referred to as an "iron horse" during the time period.)

Step 2. Literary Analysis Wheel, separate elements. Lead students through a simple analysis by completing the separate parts of the wheel.

- **Setting:** What is the setting? What words are used to describe the setting?
- **Character:** Considering the train as a character, what are the train's values and motives? (Sample response: The train is the "iron horse," which is proud and powerful, changing the landscape to fit its own needs. The train's values are to be efficient and strong, with a motivation to arrive punctually at its destination.)
- **Point of View:** What is Dickinson's point of view toward the object? How do you know? (Sample response: She sees both the negative and positive qualities.) (*Note:* Because this is a poem, we are considering the author's point of view—however, in short stories and novels, consider first person, third limited, omniscient, and objective point of view.)
- **Language:** Do you notice any specific figurative language or sound devices throughout the poem? (Sample response: Alliteration: "like," "lap," "lick;" "stop," "step;" personification: "lick," "stop," "feed itself;" simile: "neigh like Boangeres;" rhythm: unaccented-accented syllable pattern.)
- **Symbol:** What does the horse imagery represent? Why is the symbol of a horse used? How is the allusion to Boangeres a symbol? (Sample response: The horse is a symbol for the iron horse—a train. Boangeres was a vociferous disciple—loud and annoying—symbolic of the train.)
- **Tone:** What is Dickinson's attitude toward the train? What is the tone? (Sample response: Her tone is ambiguous—it is both positive and negative—she hates it but is also in awe of its power. At times her tone can also be unwelcoming and unapproving. Note how this is affected by her point of view and language.)

- **Conflict:** What is the significant conflict in the poem? (Sample response: Technology vs. nature.)
- **Theme:** What is the author's main message? (Sample response: Themes may relate to the the power of change, power of technology, or the intrusion of technology on nature.)
- **Mood:** Because this is a poem, it would be a stretch to be able to describe the mood based on the few lines that are given. It is suggested that this is not part of the poem analysis.

Step 3. Combined elements for complexity. Discuss how multiple elements interact to establish an overall interpretation of the poem.

- *How does Dickinson's use of language help develop our understanding of the character and the narrator's point of view?* She uses both positive ("docile," "omnipotent") and negative ("horrid," "Boangeres," "supercilious") connotations to show an ambiguous point of view—she loves and hates the train at the same time. The positive and negative connotations about the character help establish Dickinson's point of view.
- *How does the use of language help develop symbolism?* The horse imagery ("neigh," "feed itself at tanks," "stable") establishes the idea of "the iron horse." The *st-* alliteration helps create the sound a horse might make. The rhythm of the poem almost sounds like a train. The entire poem is a metaphor (horse compared to train) and supported through similes (e.g., "neigh like Boangeres") and personification ("lick the valleys," "feed itself," "step").
- *How does setting help establish our understanding of the train's character? How does the setting help us understand the conflict?* The train can be considered as the main character, the "iron horse," who is proud and powerful, changing the landscape to fit its own needs. It pares a quarry to meet its own needs. The use of "shanties" in the setting implies how the train condescendingly looks down upon human things. The train "licks" the valleys up, revealing how it authoritatively takes layers off the landscape.
- *How does the tone and conflict establish the theme of the poem?* Dickinson's tone and attitude toward the new technology establishes the conflict of nature versus technology. This clearly establishes the theme of the power and intrusion of technology on our lives.
- *If Dickinson were to change the theme to "overcoming obstacles," how would this affect how she describes the setting and character?* The character (the train) would be described more positively or even heroic. The setting would not showcase the train's domination; rather, it might be a hindrance to a train. Consider how the story "The Little Engine That Could" shows a contrasting theme (e.g., the setting poses an obstacle for the train instead of

the train imposing on nature; rather than the train having "power" over the setting, the setting poses "power" over the train).

VISUAL ANALYSIS WHEEL INSTRUCTIONS

The Visual Analysis Model is used to guide students through analyzing how an artist develops a main idea in art. Students analyze specific techniques, organization, and the artist's point of view toward the idea. Additionally, students examine prominent images and symbolism, the author's background, and emotions portrayed and evoked in the art. The model allows students to see the connection between multiple concepts (e.g., images are organized intentionally to create the main idea, point of view is influenced by the artist's background, specific techniques are used to evoke emotion, etc.).

Using the Visual Analysis Wheel

The Visual Analysis Wheel can be used to guide student through an in-depth analysis of art or visual media. It is meant to be interactive. The inner circle conceptually spins so that it interacts with elements on the outer circle.

The Visual Analysis Wheel Guide (Appendix B) shows specific prompts to guide students in thinking through each separate element. The teacher may simply refer to the model during instruction or students may take notes on the Blank Visual Analysis Wheel using arrows to show how the elements relate. It is suggested that students first note the answers to each concept separately on the graphic organizer, and then discuss how they influence each other.

Students can make their own interactive paper-plate model of the wheel. Two different colored papers may be used for the inner and outer circles, secured with a brass paper fastener. Students may use the wheels as visuals in small groups.

Sample questions for visual analysis. The following questions can be asked for analyzing art. Note that complexity is added by combining different elements.

Purpose:
- *What is the purpose of the art?*

Context:
- *What year was this art created? What artistic movements may have influenced this work? What type of art is this? What historical events are happening at the time this was made? Is there a specific audience for which the art was created?*

Main Idea/Message:
- *What is the main idea of this art? What is the message of the art?*

Techniques:
- *What specific techniques does the artist use? (Consider color, shape, brushstroke, patterns, contrast.)*

Point of View/Assumptions:
- *What is the artist's point of view toward the topic?*
- *What assumptions does the artist make?*
- *What is the artist's unstated premise or belief? What does the artist take for granted about the audience?*

Structure:
- *How does the artist organize ideas?*
- *What is the central part of the painting?*
- *Where is your eye drawn first? Why?*

Images/Symbols:
- *What are the main images?*
- *Do they symbolize a deeper meaning? How?*

Images/Structure:
- *Why does the artist intentionally place the objects where they are?*

Images/Point of View/Assumptions:
- *What do the artist's images reveal about his or her point of view/assumptions about the topic displayed?*

Images/Techniques:
- *What specific techniques does the artist use to create the main images of the art?*

Images/Purpose/Context:
- *How does the historical context influence the artist's choice of images in his art?*
- *How does the audience for which this is intended influence the artist's choice of images?*

Emotions:
- *What emotions does this art evoke in you?*
- *What emotions does this art reveal/portray?*

Emotions/Point of View/Assumptions:
- *How does the artist's point of view toward the topic influence your emotional reaction to the art?*

Emotions/Technique:
- *What techniques does the artist use to portray and evoke emotion from his or her art?*

Emotions/Structure:
- *Are parts of the art more emotionally powerful than others? How did the artist organize his or her painting to evoke or portray emotion?*

Emotions/Purpose/Context:
- *How does the historical situation influence how the artist expresses or evokes emotion?*

Artist Background:
- *What do you know about the artist's personal life? Who influenced his or her work? How did his or her work influence others?*

Artist Background/Technique:
- *What techniques does the artist use that are unique to his or her style?*

Artist Background/Point of View/Assumptions:
- *How does the artist's background influence his or her point of view/ assumptions about the topic?*

Artist Background/Structure:
- *Does the artist's background influence the way he or she organizes his or her art?*

Artist Background/Purpose/Context:
- *How is the artist influenced by the historical context of his or her time? How does the artist influence the historical context of his or her time?*

Implications:
- *What are the short- and long-term consequences of this art?*
- *What are the implications for you after viewing this art?*

Evaluation:
- *Do you like this art? Why or why not? Use specific elements for the wheel in your answer.*
- *What does this art make you think? Would you hang this in your home? Why or why not?*
- *What elements of this art are most important to consider and why?*

Example Visual Analysis Lesson

Students view the lithograph "Relativity" by M. C. Escher (available online). Do not reveal the title.

Step 1: Close viewing questions. Lead students through an initial viewing of the art.

- What detail of this art is interesting to you? (Ask every student; short response.)
- How many staircases are there? (Sample response: Seven; some overlap.)
- How many sources of gravity are in this picture? (Sample response: Three.)
- What behaviors do you see of the people?
- What is the focal point of the picture? Justify your answer.
- How does Escher produce "dual effects" on this painting? (Sample response: The ceiling is also a floor.) Note that though two people may be on the same staircase, they exist in two separate dimensions. Do they know of each other's existence? (Sample response: One is going up, one is going down, but they are going in the same direction.)
- Round-robin: If you had to give the lithograph a title, what title would you give it? (Ask every student; short response.)
- Share with your neighbor why you chose this title (or if time permits, elicit this as whole group).
- Share the real title of the lithograph. "Relativity." Why do you think Escher gave it this title?

Step 2. Visual Analysis Wheel, separate elements. Lead students through completing relevant parts of the Visual Analysis Wheel during discussion. Focus first on the separate elements.

- **Purpose/Context:**
  - *What is the context of this art?* Lithograph printed in 1953.
  - *What do you think his purpose/motive is in creating this?* To express an idea of reality. (*Note:* Students may not be able to determine this until after discussing the art to some extent.)

Point of View/Assumptions:

- *What is Escher's point of view toward reality?* Escher is revealing that there are multiple experiences and perceptions of reality. People perceive reality differently.

Images:

- *What do you believe are the most prominent images in the picture? Why? How might they be symbols for something deeper?* Staircases = journey in life; featureless people = unaware people, emotionless; windows to outside = ways to get out of isolation.

Emotions:

- *What emotions does this evoke in you? What emotions are revealed?* The featureless people reveal a lack of emotion, indicating that people are coming and going in life in an emotionless state.

Artist Background:

- *What do you know about the artist's background? How is the artist influenced by the historical context of his time?* M. C. Escher (1898–1972) was a famous 20th-century Dutch artist who is known for developing impossible structures within his art. He made more than 448 lithographs (original prints) and woodcarvings, and more than 2,000 drawings. Escher also wrote many poems and essays, and he studied architecture, though he never graduated from high school. He used many mathematical aspects in his works. Most of Escher's works involve his own fascination with the concept of reality. His works showing paradoxes, tessellations, and impossible objects have had influence on graphic art, psychology, philosophy, and logic.

Main Idea:

- *What is Escher conveying about life in this painting? What is Escher's main idea?* Each person has his or her own view of reality and may be unaware of others' realities.

Implications:

- *What are the implications of this art on you the viewer?*

Evaluation:

- *Do you like this art? Would you hang it in your home? Does it make you think? Was the artist successful in presenting his ideas? Justify your answers with evidence.*

Step 3. Combined elements for complexity. Combine elements to develop more complex questions. Students may draw arrows on their wheels to show how elements relate (images + techniques, etc.).

- **Images/Techniques:**
  - *What techniques does Escher use to enhance images?* The people are all identical and featureless. There are three sources of gravity and six staircases. The outside world is park-like. Some appear to be climbing upside down, but according to their gravity, they are climbing the staircase normally. Parts of the picture look two-dimensional, other parts look three-dimensional. He includes paradoxes (two people standing on same staircase in separate realities). The basements add a surreal effect.

- **Images/Structure:**
  - *How does Escher intentionally place the objects in the painting to reveal meaning?* He purposefully draws two people standing on the same step (top center); they coexist yet they are in different gravity worlds. *What does this reveal about life?* We are preoccupied with our own journeys, we do not acknowledge others' points of view.

- **Artist Background/Technique:**
  - *What techniques does Escher use that are unique to his style?* Escher creates impossible realities within this work (three gravity worlds existing as one). He is known for creating paradoxes in his art.

- **Emotions/Structure/Technique:**
  - *How did the artist organize his art to portray or evoke emotion? What techniques were used to evoke or portray emotion?* It is interesting that the staircase structure is an upside-down triangle. Perhaps this is to give a more chaotic feel to the picture. Those within the staircases are "lost" in a world of coming and going, living life unaware beyond their own self-centered world. His technique of painting featureless people portrays a lack of emotion. The lack of emotion interplays with a main idea that the people are not aware of each other's existence, particularly in the other gravity worlds.

RHETORICAL ANALYSIS WHEEL INSTRUCTIONS

The Rhetorical Analysis Model is used to analyze how an author develops and supports an argument. Students examine how a writer achieves his or her purpose by analyzing how several elements work together to create an effective argument. This includes thinking about the rhetorical situation (e.g., purpose, context, audience), means of persuasion (e.g., ethos, logos, and pathos appeals), and rhetorical strategies (e.g., techniques, evidence, structure, etc.). The author develops a claim through the use of three rhetorical appeals: logos (reasoning), pathos (emotion), and ethos (credibility) in response to the situation. These rhetorical appeals are developed by point of view, specific strategies, techniques, and organization. The model allows students to see connections between multiple elements (e.g., credibility is influenced by point of view, specific techniques are used to evoke emotion, structure develops strong logos appeals, etc.).

Overview of Aristotle's Rhetorical Appeals

Aristotle's rhetoric includes logos, ethos, and pathos appeals. This enhances a writer's ability to persuade an audience.

- **Logos:** How the author establishes good reasoning to make his message make sense. This includes major points, use of evidence, syllogisms, examples, evidence, facts, statistics, etc. Text focused.
- **Pathos:** How the author appeals to the audience's emotion. Audience focused.
- **Ethos:** How the author develops credibility and trust. Author focused.

Using the Rhetorical Analysis Wheel

The Rhetorical Analysis Wheel can be used to analyze how an author develops a claim through rhetorical appeals, techniques, and structure. Students also think through the point of view, assumptions, purpose, and implications of the document. It is meant to be interactive. The inner circle conceptually spins so that it interacts with elements on the outer circle.

The Rhetorical Analysis Wheel Guide (Appendix B) shows specific prompts to guide students in thinking through each separate element. The teacher may simply refer to the model during instruction or students may take notes on the Blank Rhetorical Analysis Wheel using arrows to show how elements relate. It is suggested that students first note the answers to each element separately on the graphic organizer, and then discuss how they influence each other. Consider making a poster of the Rhetorical Analysis Wheel Guide to refer to throughout the unit.

Students can make their own interactive paper-plate model of the wheel. Two different colored papers may be used for the inner and outer circles, secured with a brass paper fastener. Students may use the wheels as visuals in small groups.

Sample questions for rhetorical analysis. The following questions can be asked for analyzing argument. Note that complexity is added by combining elements.

Purpose:
- *What is the author's purpose?*

Context/Audience:
- *Who is the audience and what is the historical situation?*
- *What is the main problem in the historical context?*

Claim:
- *What is the main claim or message of the text?*

Techniques:
- *What specific techniques does the writer use to develop his or her claim?* Here are some examples of specific techniques that may be asked:
  - **Language:** Consider how specific word choice and style develops tone.
  - **Positive and negative connotations of words:** Consider how words evoke feelings.
  - **Personification:** Human qualities given to nonhuman objects/ ideas.
  - **Simile:** A figure of speech that compares two unlike things using "like" or "as."
  - **Metaphor:** A direct comparison between two unlike things.
  - **Hyperbole:** An extreme exaggeration.
  - **Allusion:** A reference to a historical or Biblical work, person, or event. The writer assumes the reader can make connections between the allusion and text being read.
  - **Imagery:** Formation of mental images that appeal to the senses.
  - **Parallelism:** Using similar grammatical structures in order to emphasize related ideas.
  - **Repetition:** Repeating the same wording for emphasis, clarity, or emotional impact.
  - **Contrast:** A striking difference of ideas for effect.
  - **Rhetorical question:** A question asked by the writer, but not expected to be answered aloud. It evokes reflection.
  - **Liberty rhetoric:** Using patriotic appeals for freedom.
  - **War rhetoric:** Reasoning to convince war is necessary.
  - **Syllogism:** A form of deductive logic—a conclusion drawn from two premises. Example: If x=y and y=z, then x=z. If citizens can vote and if women are citizens, then women should be allowed to vote.

♦ **Use of evidence, facts, statistics, examples, and counterclaims (strongly connects with logos):** Explicit support for the argument.

Point of View/Assumptions:
- *What is the writer's point of view toward the topic?*
- *What assumptions does the writer make?*
- *What is the writer's unstated premise or belief? What does the writer take for granted about the audience?*

Structure/Organization:
- *How does the writer organize ideas (e.g., problem-solution, point by point, chronologically, sequentially, compare/contrast)?*
- *Where is the thesis? Why is it here?*
- *Does the writer structure his or her message deductively or inductively?*

Logos (Focus on Text):
- *What reasoning is used to help the argument make sense? What are the main points?*
- *Are statements easy to accept or does the writer need to provide more evidence?*
- *What research, facts, statistics, or expert opinions are used? Are these sufficient?*
- **Logos/Structure**
  - ♦ *How does the structure of the document help the writer's argument make sense?*

- **Logos/Point of View:**
  - ♦ *Does the writer assume that the audience already accepts a premise?*
  - ♦ *What do the writer's examples and facts (or lack of) reveal about his or her assumptions about the audience?*

- **Logos/Techniques:**
  - ♦ *Which techniques are used to help the writer logically form his or her argument (e.g., syllogisms, comparisons, parallelisms, use of statistics, examples, etc.)?*

- **Logos/Context:**
  - ♦ *How do the problem, context, and audience influence the writer's approach in developing a logical argument? Because the historical situation is what it is, how does this influence the way the writer organizes his reasoning?*

Pathos (Focus on Audience):

- *How does the writer appeal to the audience's emotions (guilt, fear, pride, etc.)?*
- *What word connotations or imagery does the writer use to evoke emotion in the audience?*
- *How do pathos appeals help the writer establish his claim?*
- **Pathos/Point of View:**
  - *How does the writer's tone and point of view impact the desired emotional response?*
  - *How does the writer's bias influence the desired emotional response?*

- **Pathos/Technique:**
  - *What techniques does the writer use to evoke emotion among the audience (e.g., repetition, liberty rhetoric, war rhetoric, similes, hyperbole, symbolism, rhetorical questions)?*

- **Pathos/Structure:**
  - *Where does the writer place the emotional appeals? Why is this important? Do pathos appeals change throughout the text? How? Why? How does this enhance or take away from the argument?*

- **Pathos/Context:**
  - *How does the historical situation/problem influence how the writer uses pathos appeals? How do pathos appeals help the writer accomplish his desired effect?*

Ethos (Focus on Writer):

- *Is the writer credible?*
- *How does the writer establish trust?*
- *Are sources credible?*
- *Does the writer respect an opposing viewpoint?*
- *Does the writer address counterclaims? How?*
- *How do ethos appeals help the writer establish an effective argument?*

- **Ethos/Technique:**
  - *What techniques does the writer use to establish credibility (e.g., uses reliable sources, discusses character/reputation, etc.)?*

- **Ethos/Point of View:**
  - *Does the writer's bias take away from his or her credibility?*

      ◆ *Do the writer's assumptions about the opposing point of view reduce his or her credibility?*

- **Ethos/Structure:**
  - ◆ *Where in the document does the writer develop his or her credibility? Why is it significant he or she places his or her ethos appeals here?*
  - ◆ *Where does the writer address counterclaims? How does he or she address the counterclaim, and how does this enhance or reduce his or her credibility?*

- **Ethos/Context:**
  - ◆ *Why is it important for the writer to develop trust with this audience in this historical situation?*
  - ◆ *What must the writer consider about the audience when establishing his or her credibility?*

Implications:
- *What are the short- and long-term implications/consequences of this document?*

Evaluation:
- *How effective is the writer in developing his or her claim? To what extent is the purpose fulfilled?*
- *Is there a balance of pathos, ethos, and logos appeals?*
- *Is there too much bias or emotional manipulation? Is there adequate evidence to support the claim(s)? Is the evidence credible, rational, and organized logically?*

Students should consider the author's purpose (to entertain, inform, persuade, express) when determining how effective the argument is. For example, it may not be necessary to provide counterarguments if the purpose of the text is not to persuade. Students should also consider the balance of logos, ethos, and pathos appeals.

Example Rhetorical Analysis Lesson

Students should read the excerpt from Franklin D. Roosevelt's Second Inaugural Address (see p. 184).

Step 1: Text-dependent questions. Lead students through a close reading of the text for initial comprehension. You may also ask students to paraphrase sections of the text into their own words.

    According to Roosevelt, what brings an ever richer life to Americans?

- Why does Roosevelt personify Comfort, Opportunism, and Timidity? How are these "voices" considered distractions?
- What are some of the positive aspects of the current state of affairs?
- According to the text, why is prosperity dangerous?
- What is meant by "prosperity already tests the persistence of our progressive purpose"?
- Which one of Roosevelt's "I see" statements is most powerful?
- According to the text, how do we test our progress?
- What is Roosevelt's solution to the problems of tens of millions?
- What four words are most important to the text? Can you put these four words together in a sentence to summarize FDR's main message?

Step 2: Teach elements of rhetorical analysis. Teach students some basic principles of a rhetorical analysis:

- **Modes of Rhetoric (Logos, Pathos, Ethos):** Explain Aristotle's modes of rhetoric (see p. 174).
- **Techniques:** Students will consider how these appeals are developed through different techniques used by the author. Go over a few techniques with students (see p. 175). Note that language, positive and negative connotations, personification, repetition, and rhetorical questions are used.
- **Structure/Organization:** Students should consider where the appeals are placed within the documents and why they are there. They should also consider the overall structure of the document as it often supports the logos appeal (it helps the author's rationale "make sense" by putting ideas in this order). Why is it important that the points are placed structurally where they are? Throughout the analysis, the elements of logos, ethos, and pathos interact with structure, techniques and point of view.

Step 3: Rhetorical Analysis Wheel: Separate Elements. Lead students through completing relevant parts of the Rhetorical Analysis Wheel. Students do not need to write detailed explanations on the organizer, just notes. Focus first on the separate elements.

- **Purpose:**
  - *What is Roosevelt's purpose in delivering this message?* To persuade the American people to carry on toward progress by moving forward together.

- **Message/Claim:**
  - *What is Roosevelt's main claim? What is the main idea he is proving?* America will carry on toward progress by addressing concerns of all.

Point of View/Assumptions:

- *What is Roosevelt's point of view toward progress? What are his assumptions?* FDR believes Americans should cautiously handle prosperity; it can distract Americans from progressing because of the self-interest involved. He assumes that government involvement into the affairs of people is welcomed, justified, and of goodwill.

Structure:

- *What is the overall structure of the speech?* Problem-solution.

Techniques:

- *What are some techniques you notice within the speech?* Rhetorical questions, personification, etc.

Logos:

- *What are the main points? How does the author support his claim with evidence and facts? What are the main "reasons" that support the claim?* **Logos/Reasoning:** FDR notes that America has progressed, but not arrived, and the American people should be warned by the disasters of prosperity. He lists positive state of affairs, lists negative state of affairs, and explains a hopeful future via government involvement. He provides evidence of a negative state of affairs ("I see millions . . . ").

Pathos:

- *What emotion(s) does the author attempt to evoke in the audience (pathos)?* FDR appeals to a sense of sympathy ("I see millions . . . ") and pride ("If I know aught of the will of our people . . . ").

Ethos:

- *Is the author credible? How does the author establish trust? Is evidence credible?* FDR is speaking at his second inaugural address and acknowledges the progress made during his presidency. He also refers to the government as effective and competent to build trust. Evidence is not supported with specific credibility, and he is somewhat biased with his enthusiasm for a competent government addressing problems.

Implications:

- *What are the short- and long-term implications/consequences of this document?* This speech set the stage for many of FDR's initiatives. During his second term, Congress passed the Housing Act, laws were made to establish minimum wage (Fair Labor Standards Act), and more than 3.3 million jobs were developed through WPA (Works Progress Administration).

Step 4: Combined elements for complexity. Combine elements to develop more complex questions. Students may draw arrows on their wheels to show how elements relate (pathos + techniques, etc.).

- **Logos/Techniques:**
  - *What techniques are used to develop the reasoning in his argument?* He sets up the first point by asking a rhetorical question ("Shall we pause now and turn our back . . . "), uses personification to introduce the idea that we should be warned by the disasters of prosperity ("Comfort says . . . timidity says . . . "), addresses a counterclaim and acknowledges that we have progressed ("true, we have come far . . . "), and explains how progress today is more difficult in light of prosperity.

- **Logos/Structure:**
  - *How is the argument structured logically?* Problem-solution. It is also organized inductively. His main claim is that Americans will carry on by addressing the concerns of all. He provides evidence first and then makes this claim.

- **Pathos/Techniques:**
  - *What techniques are used to develop pathos appeals?* He uses repetition ("I see millions . . . ") to develop sympathy. He develops a sense of urgency with "at this very moment . . . " He uses loaded language ("meager," "indecent," "poverty," "denying work," "ill-housed," "ill-clad," "ill-nourished") for sympathy and pride ("goodwill," "effective government," "uncorrupted by cancers of injustice," "strong," "will to peace," "long-cherished ideals").

- **Pathos/Structure:**
  - *Where does he place pathos appeals (structure)? Why? Do they change? Why?* The pathos appeals are in line with the problem-solution logos structure. As he develops the problem, he evokes sympathy. As he develops the solution, he evokes pride.

- **Ethos/Techniques/Structure:**
  - *What techniques are used to establish ethos appeals and why are they placed where they are?* He includes "we," and "us" throughout the speech to connect with the audience. As he uses "we," he establishes that he has been a part of the present gains. The "we" language shifts to "I"—reveal-

ing that the audience can really trust him because he himself sees the problems. He shifts again to "we" when connecting the audience to the goodwill of the nation.

Evaluation:
- *How effective is the author in supporting his claim? Is there a balance of pathos, ethos, and logos appeals? Is the claim fully supported?* Roosevelt is effective in supporting the claim that America will continue on toward progress by addressing the concerns of all. There is a balance of logos, ethos, and pathos appeals. FDR gives sufficient evidence of the problem with the repeated "I see" statements, though the credibility of this evidence is not specific, but general.

Text Analysis Example, Simplified Version

Some teachers of younger grades may wish to focus on how the author supports a central idea by using relevant and sufficient evidence. This model does not focus on the rhetorical appeals (logos, ethos, and pathos) to support a claim, rather it focuses on why the author chose to use specific points to advance a central idea.

The following are simple and complex questions that could be used:

Purpose:
- *What is Roosevelt's purpose in delivering this message?* To persuade the American people to carry on toward progress by moving forward together.

Central Idea:
- *What is FDR's central idea (main message)?* We will carry on toward progress by addressing the concerns of all.

Point of View/Assumptions:
- *What is FDR's point of view toward progress? What are his assumptions?* FDR believes Americans should cautiously handle prosperity; it can distract us from progressing because of the self-interest involved. He assumes that government involvement into the affairs of people is welcomed, justified, and of goodwill.

Point 1/Evidence:
- *What is one important point FDR makes to develop his central idea?* **Point 1:** We should we warned by the disasters of prosperity. **Evidence:** "Comfort says, 'tarry a while.' Opportunism . . . ' To hold progress today, however, is more difficult . . . . "

- *How does this point develop his central idea?* This explains the state of affairs—the nation has made great progress and experienced prosperity, but prosperity can also present a problem. He asks the nation to consider the nature of progress.
- *What techniques are used to develop this point?* He personifies comfort, opportunism, and timidity to explain that the nation is at a place of decision in the face of prosperity. He describes symptoms of prosperity with negative word connotations ("dulled conscience, irresponsibility . . .").
- *Why is it important the author discusses this point at this particular part of the speech (structure)?* This allows him to introduce the problem of prosperity. This sets him up to explain to the audience that not everyone is reaping the benefits of prosperity, which is important in developing his central idea.

Point 2/Evidence:
- *What is another important point FDR uses to develop his central idea?* **Point 2:** He explains a negative state of affairs. **Evidence:** "I see millions . . . ill-housed, ill-clad, ill-nourished."
- *How does this point develop the central idea?* It explains the problem of poverty, that the concerns of all citizens are not addressed even within a time of prosperous progress.
- *What techniques are used to develop his point?* He uses both repetition ("I see millions") and loaded language ("meager," "indecent," "poverty," "denying work," "ill-housed," "ill-clad," "ill-nourished") to develop sympathy (pathos appeal).
- *Why is it important that the author discusses this point at this particular part of the speech (structure)?* At this part of the speech, he is developing the problem before he offers a solution. As he develops the problem, he evokes sympathy.

Point 3/Evidence:
- *What is another important point FDR uses to develop his central idea?* **Point 3:** FDR explains a hopeful future via government involvement. **Evidence:** "But it is not in despair I paint you that picture . . . government is competent . . . ."
- *How does this point develop the central idea?* It explains how the nation can address the concerns of all of its citizens, even those in poverty.
- *What techniques are used to develop his point? How does this technique develop his point?* He revisits the personified comfort, opportunism and timidity to remind the audience about the problem of prosperity within

his solution for more government involvement. He uses positive word connotations when referring to the government and the American people ("men and women of good will," "warm hearts of dedication," "competent," "effective"). He refers to the government as effective and competent to build trust (ethos appeal).

- *Why is this point where it is in the document (structure)? How does it help develop the central idea?* This point includes his closing where he offers a solution for the American people—come together with the government to address the problems of both comfortable prosperity and poverty.

Structure:

- *What is the overall structure of the document?* Problem-solution.

Implications:

- *What are implications/consequences of this document?* This speech set the stage for many of FDR's initiatives. During his second term, Congress passed the Housing Act, laws were made to establish minimum wage (Fair Labor Standards Act), and more than 3.3 million jobs were developed through WPA (Works Progress Administration).

Evaluation:

- *How effective is the author in using sufficient, relevant evidence to develop a central idea?* Roosevelt is somewhat effective in supporting the central idea that America will continue on toward progress by addressing the concerns of all. He speaks of the problem of progress and prosperity in general terms, but allows the audience to consider the problem through the present context. He provides a sufficient amount of evidence for stating the problems of poverty through the repetition of "I see" statements, and he effectively explains how the government and the American people can work together to address the concerns of all.

FRANKLIN D. ROOSEVELT'S SECOND INAUGURAL ADDRESS

Delivered January 20, 1937

. . . Among men of good will, science and democracy together offer an ever-richer life and ever-larger satisfaction to the individual. With this change in our moral climate and our rediscovered ability to improve our economic order, we have set our feet upon the road of enduring progress.

Shall we pause now and turn our back upon the road that lies ahead? Shall we call this the promised land? Or, shall we continue on our way? For "each age is a dream that is dying, or one that is coming to birth."

Many voices are heard as we face a great decision. Comfort says, "Tarry a while." Opportunism says, "This is a good spot." Timidity asks, "How difficult is the road ahead?"

True, we have come far from the days of stagnation and despair. Vitality has been preserved. Courage and confidence have been restored. Mental and moral horizons have been extended.

But our present gains were won under the pressure of more than ordinary circumstances. Advance became imperative under the goad of fear and suffering. The times were on the side of progress.

To hold to progress today, however, is more difficult. Dulled conscience, irresponsibility, and ruthless self-interest already reappear. Such symptoms of prosperity may become portents of disaster! Prosperity already tests the persistence of our progressive purpose.

Let us ask again: Have we reached the goal of our vision of that fourth day of March 1933? Have we found our happy valley?

I see a great nation, upon a great continent, blessed with a great wealth of natural resources. Its hundred and thirty million people are at peace among themselves; they are making their country a good neighbor among the nations. I see a United States which can demonstrate that, under democratic methods of government, national wealth can be translated into a spreading volume of human comforts hitherto unknown, and the lowest standard of living can be raised far above the level of mere subsistence.

But here is the challenge to our democracy: In this nation I see tens of millions of its citizens—a substantial part of its whole population—who at this very moment are denied the greater part of what the very lowest standards of today call the necessities of life.

I see millions of families trying to live on incomes so meager that the pall of family disaster hangs over them day by day.

I see millions whose daily lives in city and on farm continue under conditions labeled indecent by a so-called polite society half a century ago.

I see millions denied education, recreation, and the opportunity to better their lot and the lot of their children.

I see millions lacking the means to buy the products of farm and factory and by their poverty denying work and productiveness to many other millions.

I see one-third of a nation ill-housed, ill-clad, ill-nourished.

But it is not in despair that I paint you that picture. I paint it for you in hope—because the nation, seeing and understanding the injustice in it, proposes to paint it out. We are determined to make every American citizen the subject of his country's interest and concern; and we will never regard any faithful law-abiding group within our borders as superfluous. The test of our progress is not whether we add more to the abundance of those who have much; it is whether we provide enough for those who have too little.

If I know aught of the spirit and purpose of our Nation, we will not listen to comfort, opportunism, and timidity. We will carry on.

Overwhelmingly, we of the Republic are men and women of good will; men and women who have more than warm hearts of dedication; men and women who have cool heads and willing hands of practical purpose as well. They will insist that every agency of popular government use effective instruments to carry out their will.

Government is competent when all who compose it work as trustees for the whole people. It can make constant progress when it keeps abreast of all the facts. It can obtain justified support and legitimate criticism when the people receive true information of all that government does.

If I know aught of the will of our people, they will demand that these conditions of effective government shall be created and maintained. They will demand a nation uncorrupted by cancers of injustice and, therefore, strong among the nations in its example of the will to peace.

Today we reconsecrate our country to long-cherished ideals in a suddenly changed civilization. In every land there are always at work forces that drive men apart and forces that draw men together. In our personal ambitions we are individualists. But in our seeking for economic and political progress as a nation, we all go up, or else we all go down, as one people.

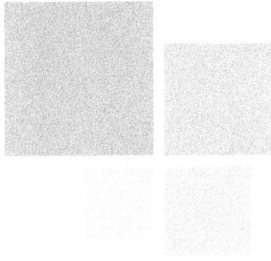

Appendix B

Blank Models and Guides

BLANK LITERARY ANALYSIS WHEEL

Directions: Draw arrows across elements to show connections.

Text: _____

Purpose/Context

Setting

Mood

Language
Structure
Style

Symbols

Plot/
Conflict

Characters

Theme

Point of View

Tone

Interpretation

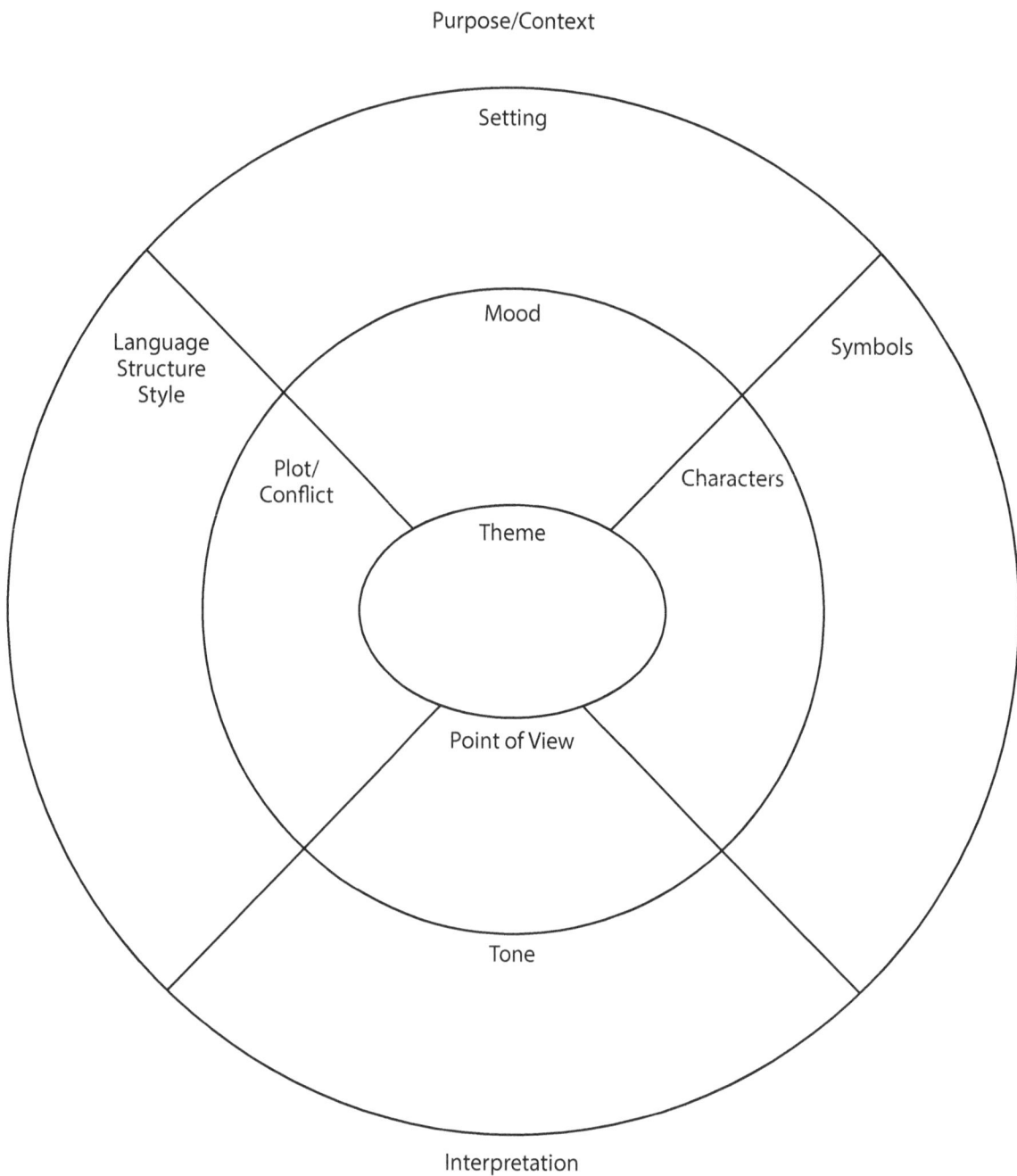

Created by Tamra Stambaugh, Ph.D., & Emily Mofield, Ed.D., 2015.

LITERARY ANALYSIS WHEEL GUIDE

Text: _____

Purpose/Context

Setting

Time, Place

Language
Structure
Style

Figurative
Language, Sound
Devices, Imagery,
Connotations,
Dialect, Writer's
Style, Sentence
Structure,
Organization of
Text

Mood

Reader's Feeling

Symbols

Abstract Meaning,
Names, Objects,
Places

Plot/
Conflict

Exposition-Climax-
Resolution, Irony,
Flashback, Internal
and External
Conflicts

Theme

Message,
Relates to Real World

Characters

Values, Motives,
Thoughts, Actions

Point of View

Narrator, First Person,
Third Person-Limited,
Objective, Omniscient

Tone

Author's Attitude,
Positive-Negative-Neutral

Interpretation

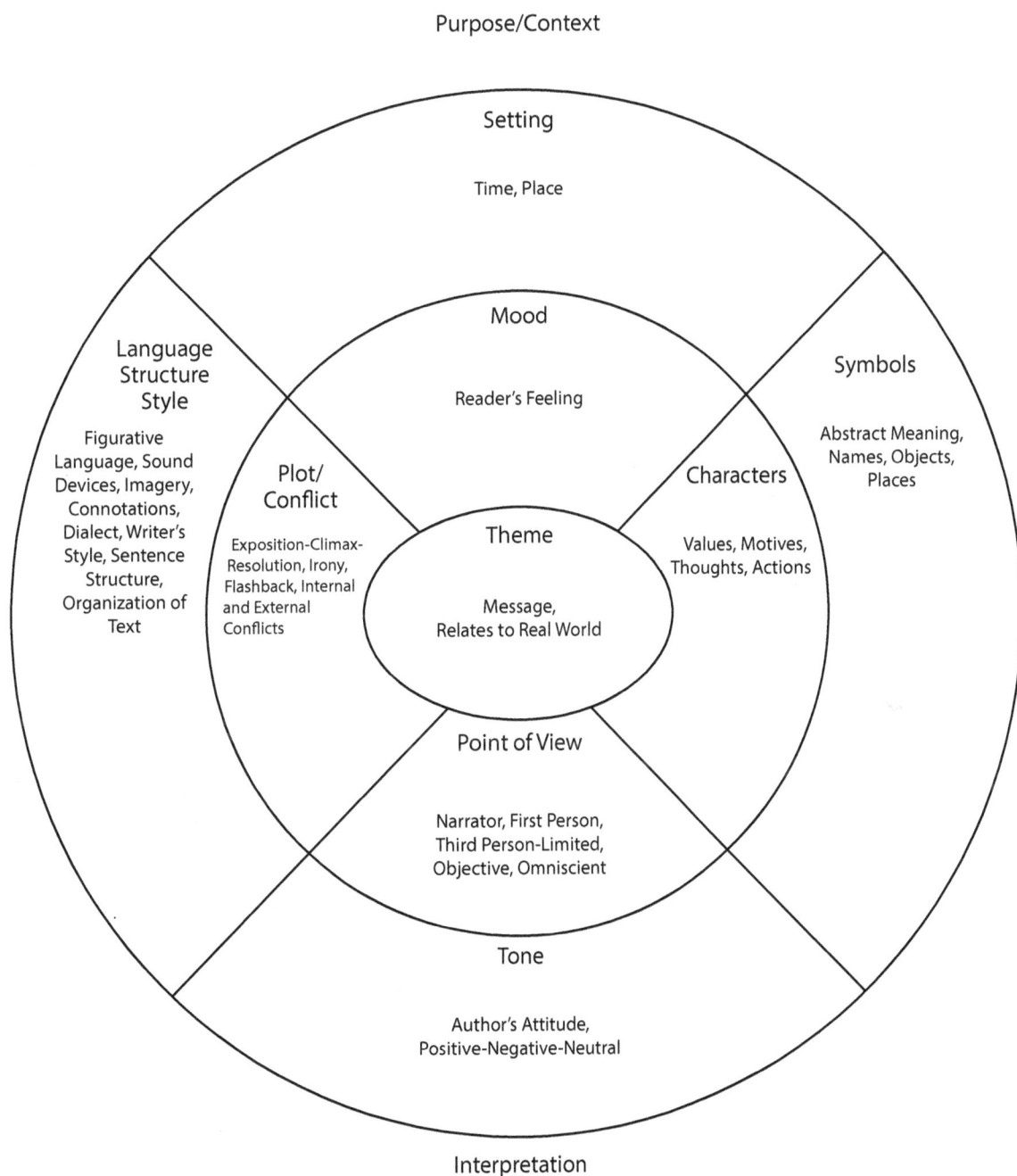

Created by Tamra Stambaugh, Ph.D., & Emily Mofield, Ed.D., 2015.

BLANK VISUAL ANALYSIS WHEEL

Directions: Draw arrows across elements to show connections.

Art Piece: _____

Purpose/Context

Point of View

Images

Techniques

Emotions

Main Idea

Artist Background

Structure/Organization

Implications

Evaluation

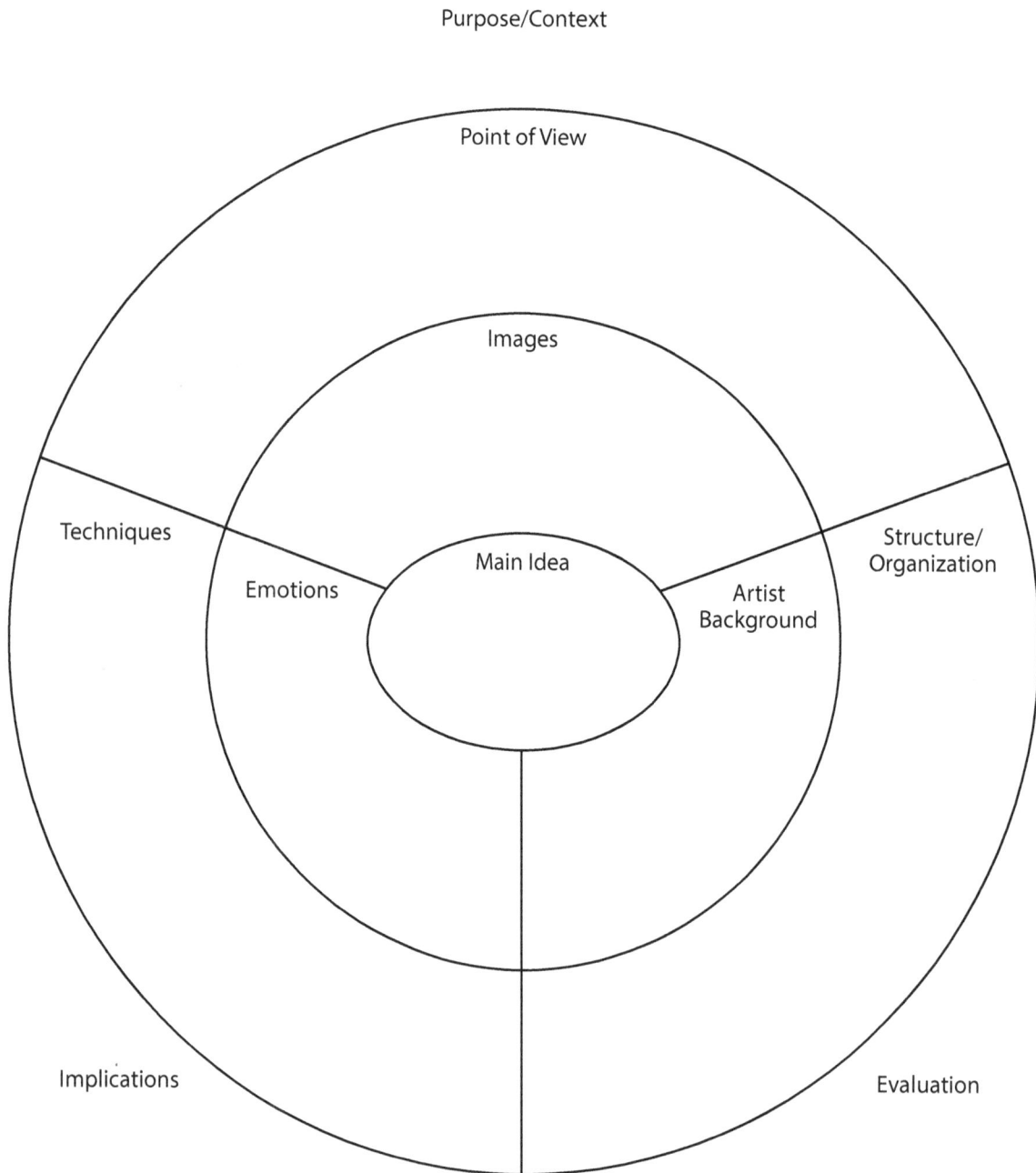

Created by Tamra Stambaugh, Ph.D., & Emily Mofield, Ed.D., 2015.

VISUAL ANALYSIS WHEEL GUIDE

Art Piece: _____

Purpose/Context

Point of View

What is the artist's point of view toward the topic?
What assumptions are made?

Images

What are the prominent images?
What might they represent?

Techniques

Visual Effects, Color, Lines, Shape, Movement, Contrast, Placement, Brush-Stroke, Pattern

Emotions

What emotions are portrayed? What emotions are evoked?

Main Idea

What is the main idea, theme, or message?

Artist Background

What is the artist's background?

Structure/ Organization

Where are your eyes drawn first? How does the placement of images influence meaning? How is the art structured?

Implications

What are the short-term and long-term implications of this art?

Evaluation

Do you like this art? Why?

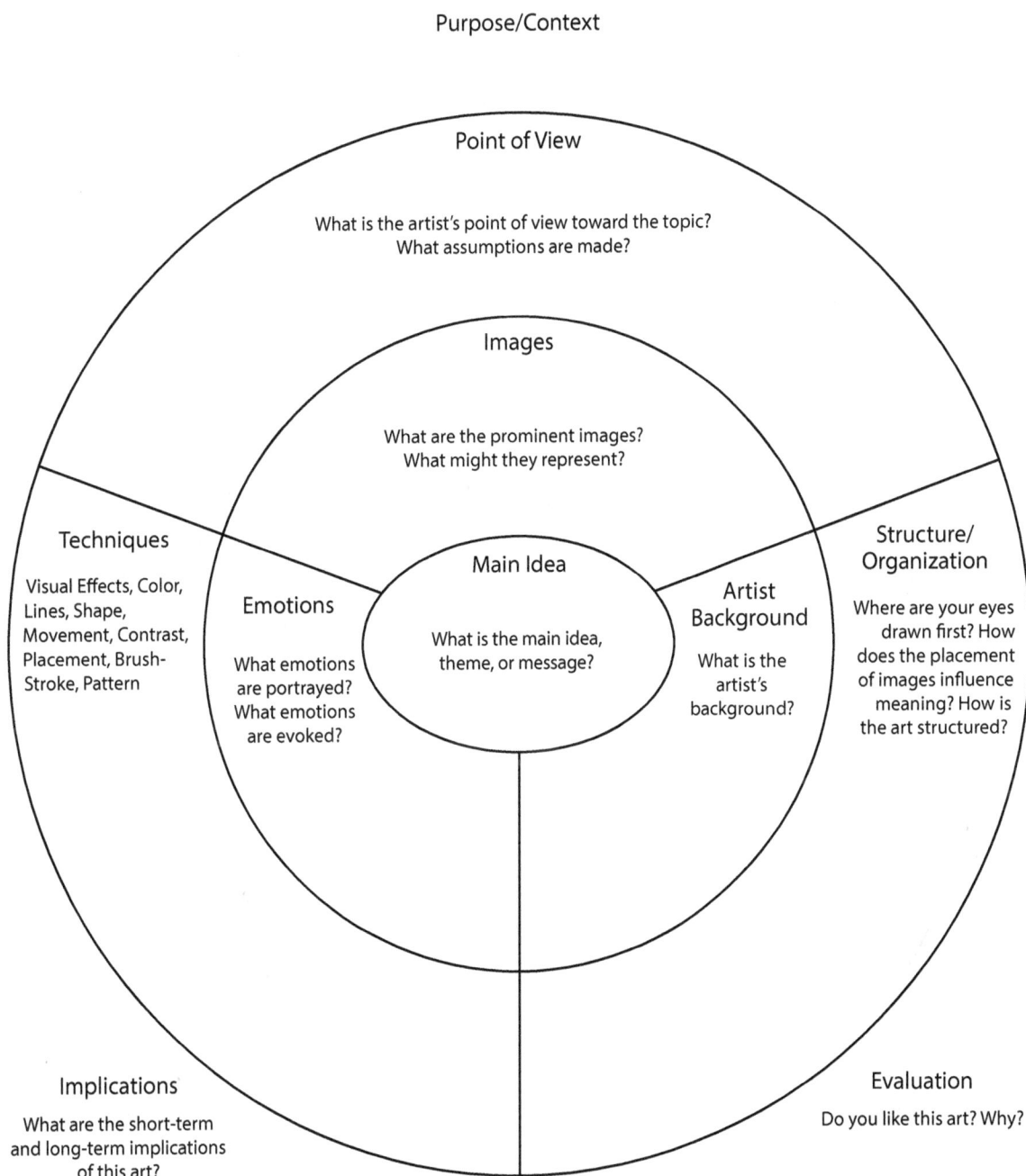

Created by Tamra Stambaugh, Ph.D., & Emily Mofield, Ed.D., 2015.

BLANK RHETORICAL ANALYSIS WHEEL

Directions: Draw arrows across elements to show connections.

Text: _____

Purpose/Context

Point of View

Logos

Techniques

Structure/
Organization

Pathos

Claim

Ethos

Implications

Evaluation

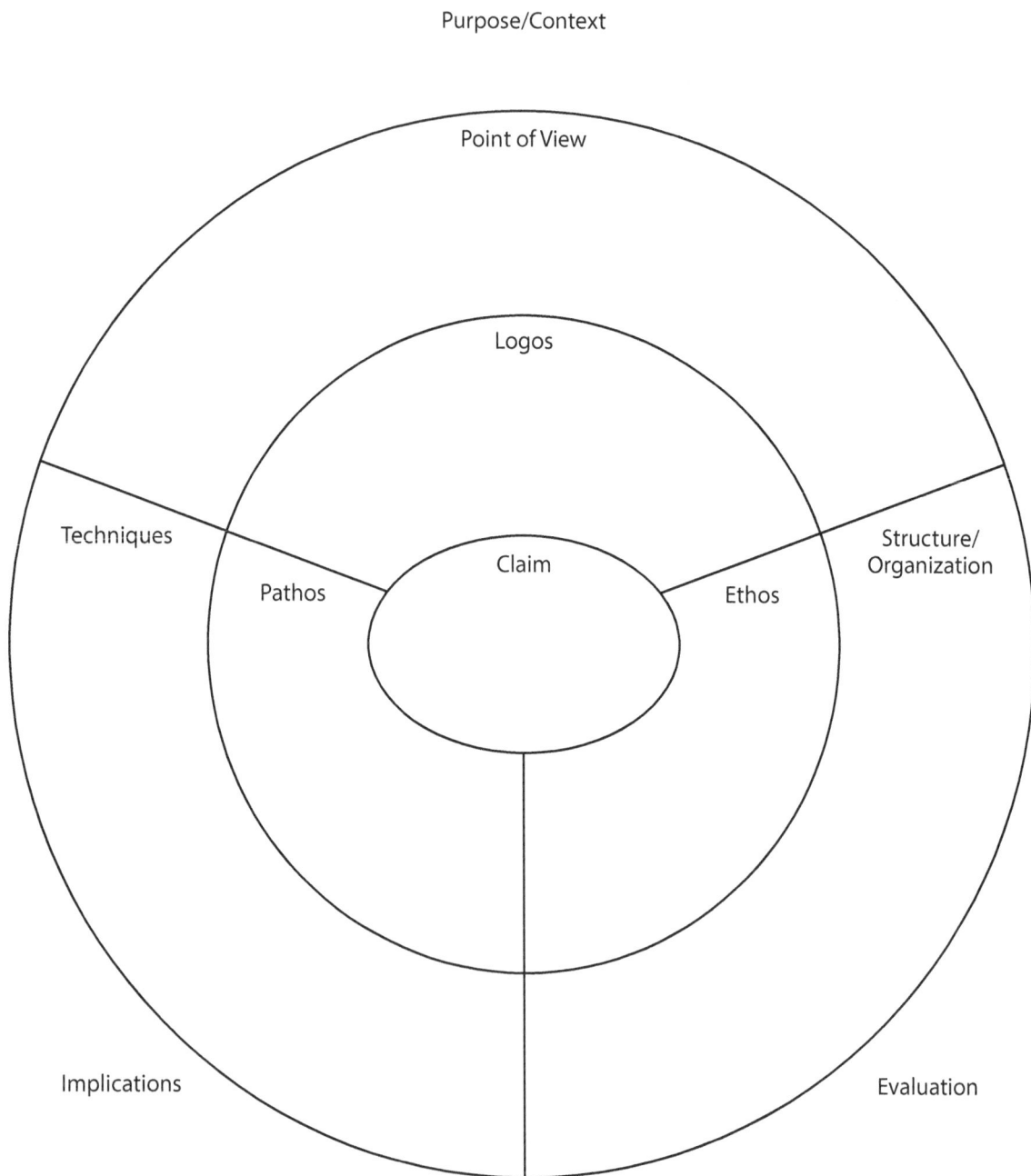

Created by Emily Mofield, Ed.D., & Tamra Stambaugh, Ph.D., 2015.

RHETORICAL ANALYSIS WHEEL GUIDE

Text: _____

Purpose/Context

What is the author's purpose? (Consider historical context.)

Key Question

How does the author develop/support the claim?

Point of View

What is the author's point of view? What assumptions are made? How does point of view establish tone? Is the author biased? Does he or she address the opposing side?

Logos

Reasons, Main Points, Examples, How the author helps the argument "make sense."

Claim

What is the claim?

Techniques

Language (Tone), +/- Connotations, Metaphor/Simile, Hyperbole, Allusion, Imagery, Parallelism, Repetition, Contrast, Analogy, Rhetorical Questions, Liberty Rhetoric, War Rhetoric, Facts, Statistics, Syllogism, Address Opposing Side

Pathos

Feelings Evoked

Ethos

Trust, Credibility

Structure/ Organization

Cause-Effect, Problem-Solution, Sequential, Chronological, Point by Point, Compare-Contrast, Inductive, Deductive

How does the author develop logos, ethos, and pathos appeals?

How are logos, ethos, and pathos organized?

Implications

What are the short-term and long-term implications of this text?

Evaluation

How effective is the author in developing his or her claim? Is there a balance of appeals?

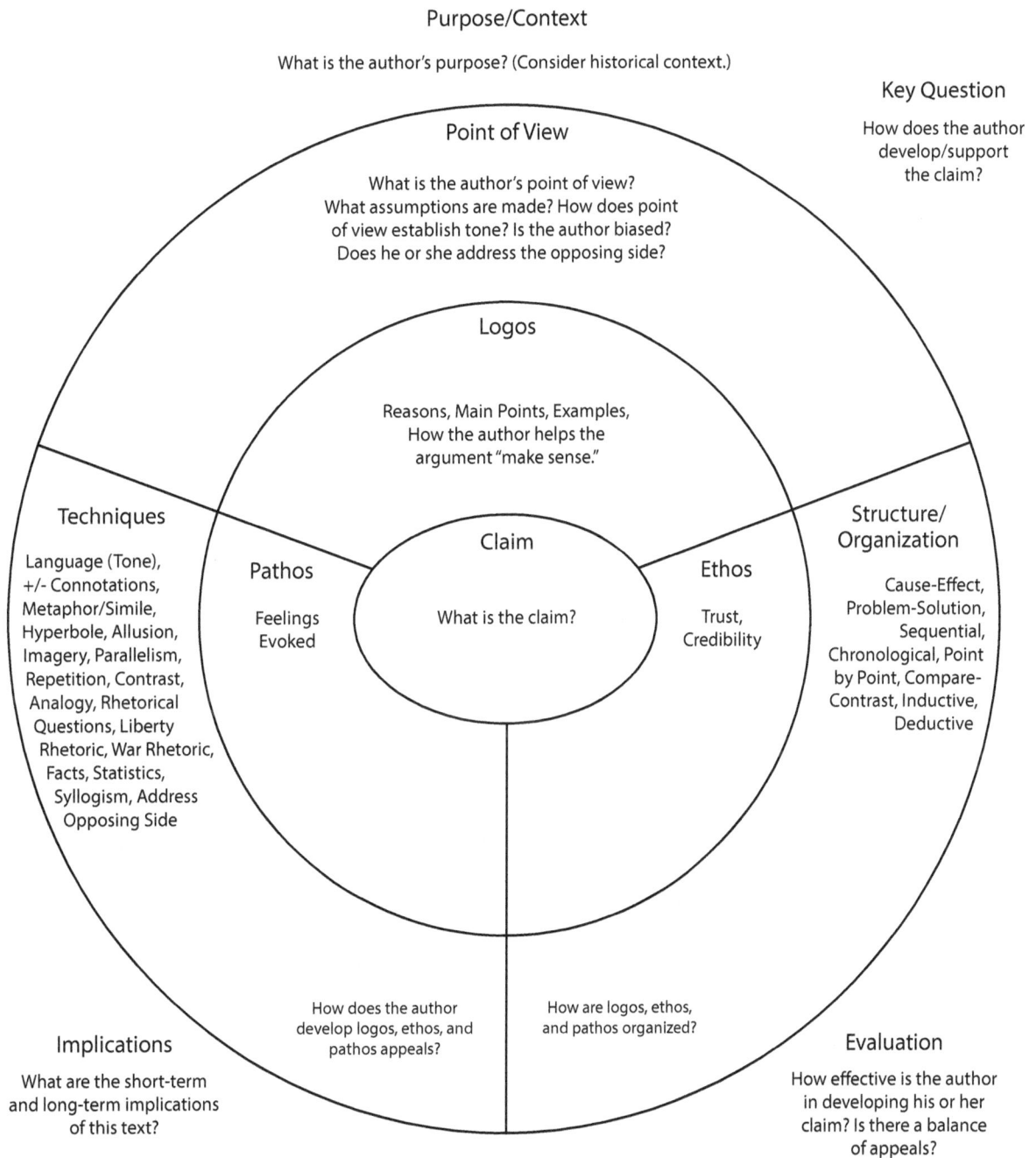

Created by Emily Mofield, Ed.D., & Tamra Stambaugh, Ph.D., 2015.

BLANK TEXT ANALYSIS WHEEL

Directions: Draw arrows across elements to show connections.

Text: _____

Purpose/Context

Point of View

Point #1

Evidence

Techniques

Central Idea

Point #2

Point #3

Structure/
Organization

Evidence

Evidence

Implications

Evaluation

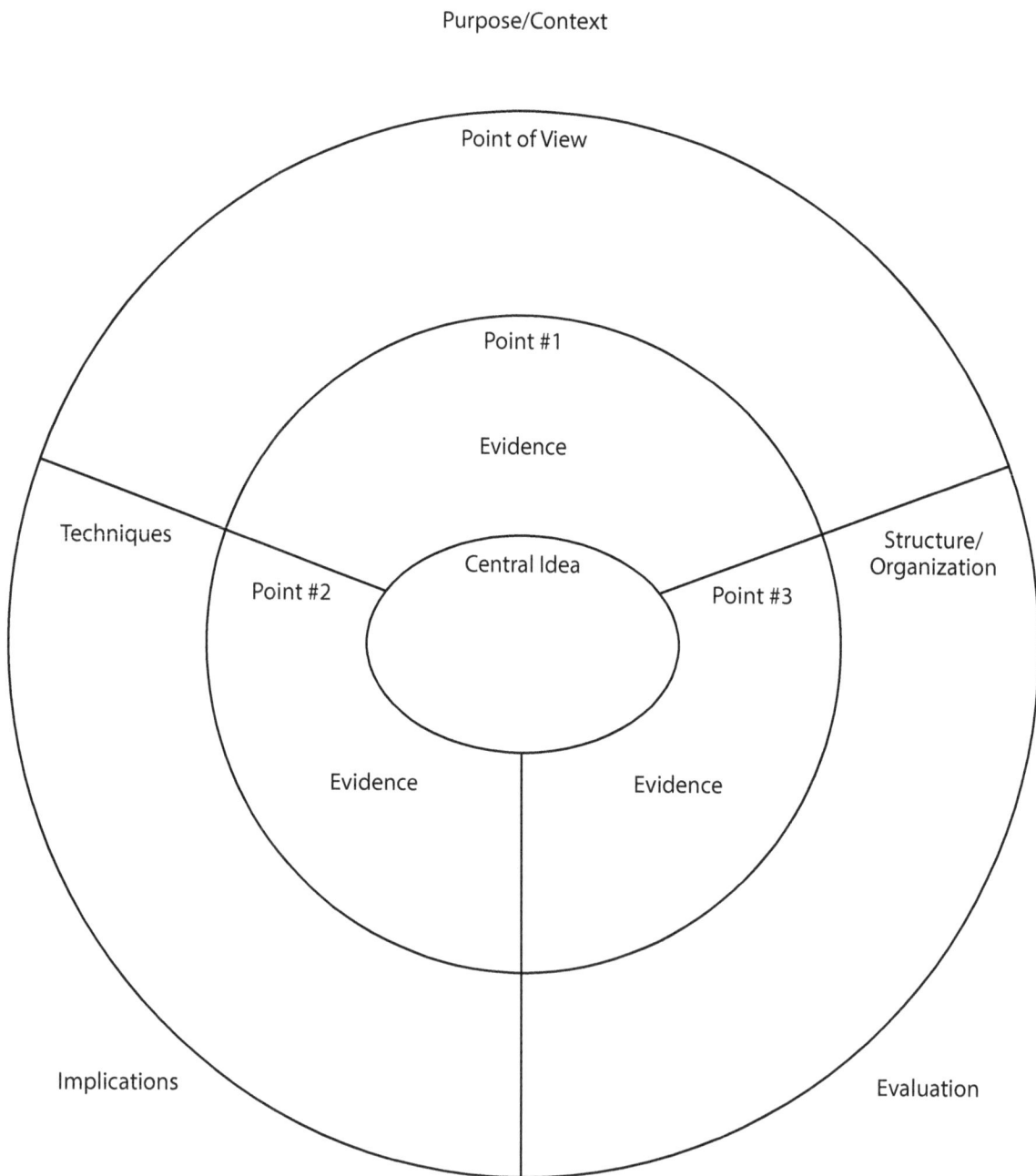

Created by Emily Mofield, Ed.D., & Tamra Stambaugh, Ph.D., 2015.

TEXT ANALYSIS WHEEL GUIDE

Text: _____

Purpose/Context

What is the author's purpose? (Consider historical context.)

Key Question

How does the author develop/support the central idea?

Point of View

What is the author's point of view? What assumptions are made? How does point of view establish tone? Is the author biased? Does he or she address the opposing side?

Point #1

What point supports the central idea? Why is this evidence important to developing the central idea?

Techniques

Language (Tone), +/- Connotations, Metaphor/Simile, Hyperbole, Allusion, Imagery, Parallelism, Repetition, Contrast, Analogy, Rhetorical Questions, Liberty Rhetoric, War Rhetoric, Facts, Statistics, Syllogism, Address Opposing Side

Point #2

What point supports the central idea? Why is this evidence important to developing the central idea?

Central Idea

What is the central idea?

Point #3

What point supports the central idea? Why is this evidence important to developing the central idea?

Structure/ Organization

Cause-Effect, Problem-Solution, Sequential, Chronological, Point by Point, Compare-Contrast, Inductive, Deductive

How does the author develop his or her points?

How are the main points organized?

Implications

What are the short-term and long-term implications of this text?

Evaluation

How effective is the author in developing his or her central idea?

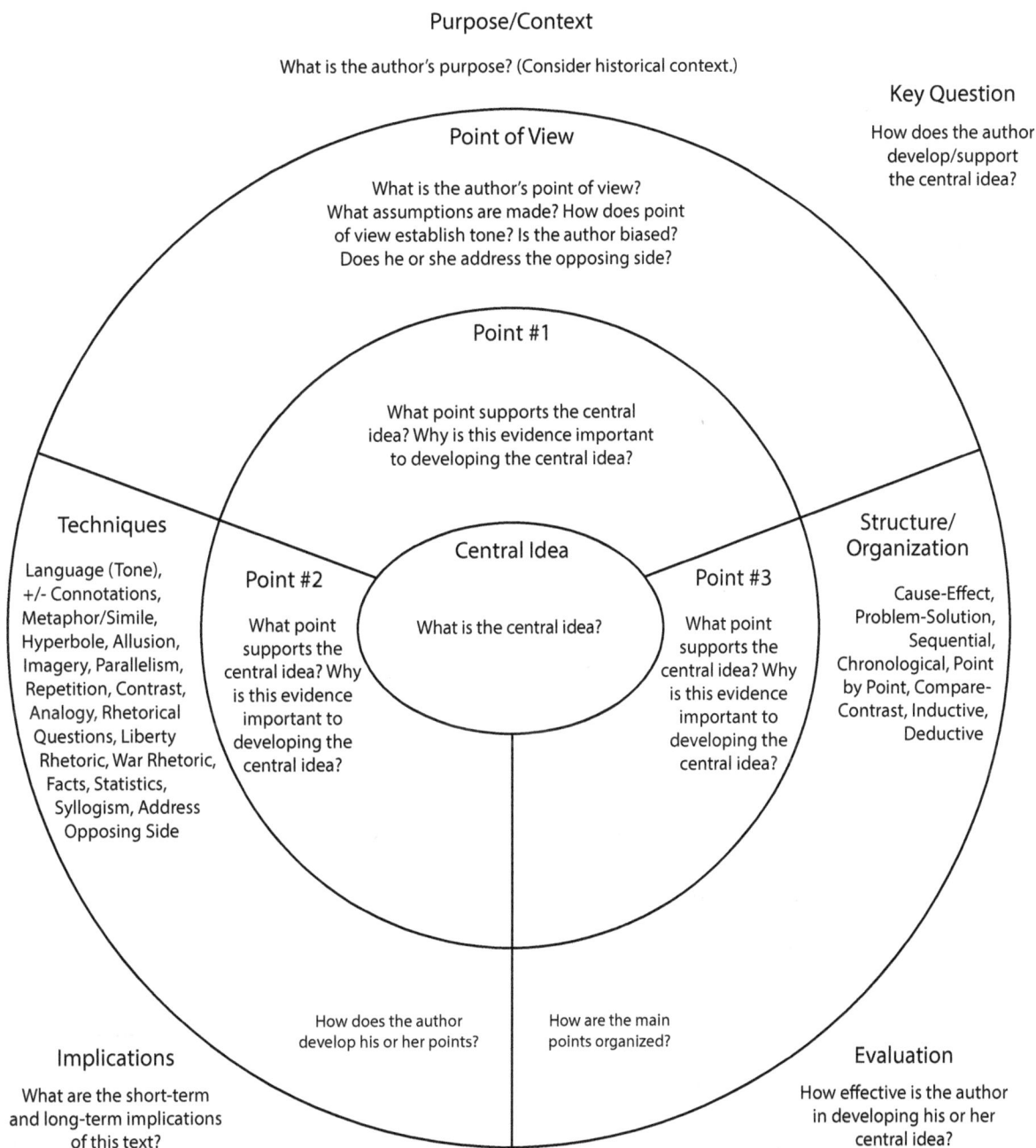

Created by Emily Mofield, Ed.D., & Tamra Stambaugh, Ph.D., 2015.

BIG IDEA REFLECTION

What?	**Concepts:** What concepts/ideas are in the text?	
	Generalizations: What broad statement can you make about one or more of these concepts? Make it generalizable beyond the text.	
	Issue: What is the main issue, problem, or conflict?	
So What?	**Insight:** What insight on life is provided from this text?	
	World/Community/Individual: How does this text relate to you, your community, or your world? What question does the author want you to ask yourself?	
Now What?	**Implications:** How should you respond to the ideas in the text? What action should you take? What are the implications of the text? What can you do with this information?	

Created by Emily Mofield, Ed.D., & Tamra Stambaugh, Ph.D., 2015.

REASONING ABOUT A SITUATION OR EVENT

What Is the Situation?

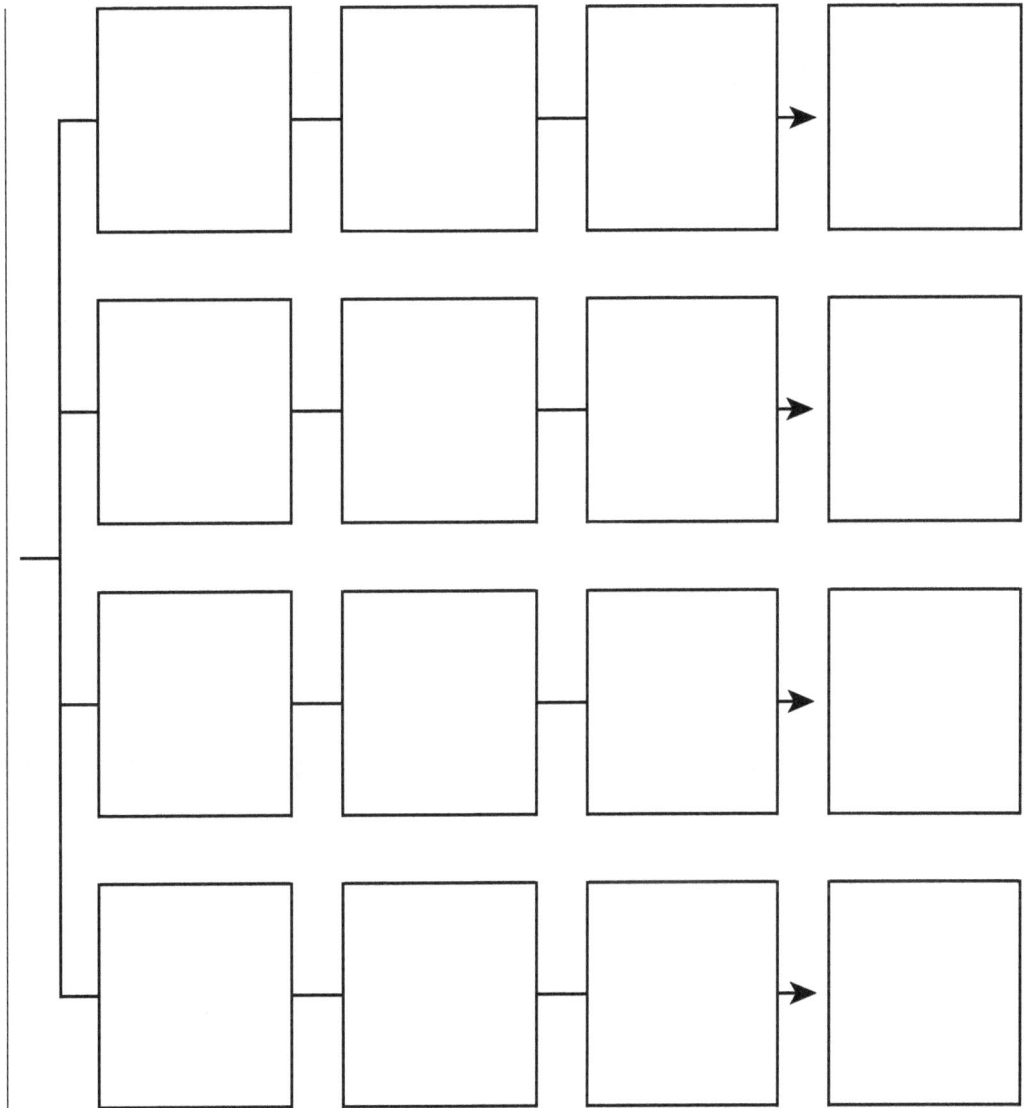

Stakeholders	Point of View	Assumptions	Implications

Adapted from "Reasoning About a Situation or Event" by Center for Gifted Education, n.d., retrieved from http://education. wm.edu/centers/cfge/curriculum/teachingmodels. Copyright 2015 by William & Mary, Center for Gifted Education.

CONCEPT ORGANIZER

Literature, Art, or Media: _____	Literature, Art, or Media: _____	Literature, Art, or Media: _____
Both conformity and individuality are agents of change.		
Both conformity and individuality involve sacrifice.		
There are positives and negatives to both conformity and individuality.		
Examine the relationship between conformity and/or individuality and another concept.		

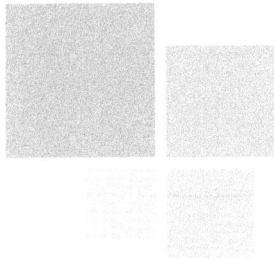

Appendix C

Rubrics

RUBRIC 1: PRODUCT RUBRIC

Name: _____   Date: _____   Lesson: _____

	Unacceptable/ Needs Improvement	Fair	Acceptable	Excellent
Completion	Not turned in or late.	Missing key pieces.	Completed but lacks thought and professionalism.	Satisfactorily meets all requirements and expectations of the task.
Content/ Concept	Limited or vague connection.	Little connection from lesson content is made to conformity themes.	Accurately relates lesson content ideas of individuality and/or conformity to assignment.	Insightfully relates the theme of individuality and/or conformity to assignment.
Thinking	Limited or vague evidence.	Reasoning is inaccurate, lacks originality, logical conclusions, or substantial claims.	Demonstrates some evidence of higher level thinking (creativity, evaluation, or analysis).	Demonstrates substantial evidence of higher level thinking (creativity, analysis, or evaluation with evidence).
Student-Developed Criteria				

Comments:

RUBRIC 2: COLLAGE RUBRIC

Name: _____ Date: _____

	Unacceptable/ Needs Improvement	Fair	Acceptable	Exemplary
All words and images are relevant to the theme and/or related text.				
The collage/media includes at least 4 quotes from newspapers, magazines, or computer-generated text supporting the theme in the text.				
Collage/media includes at least 4 quotes from text studied.				
The collage/media includes at least 8 symbolic elements representing theme.				
The images and words are arranged thoughtfully to enhance the design and layout of the collage/media.				
A written description is included explaining each symbolic element and how the pictures and quotes support a selected theme.				
The collage/media includes adequate detail about the selected theme.				
The content of the collage/media is interesting and visually appealing.				
The collage/media communicates the student's understanding of theme.				
The collage includes a creative title to support the theme and text.				
Total				

Comments:

RUBRIC 3: CULMINATING PROJECT RUBRIC

Name: _____   Date: _____

	Unacceptable/ Needs Improvement	Fair	Acceptable	Exemplary
Completion	Not turned in or late.	Missing key pieces	Completed but lacks thought and professionalism.	Satisfactorily meets all requirements and expectations of the task.
Evidence	Limited or no evidence.	Little support or elaboration to support ideas and generalizations.	Gives support/elaboration to support ideas.	Gives meaningful support/ elaboration to support ideas and generalizations.
Concept	Limited or vague connection.	Little connection from unit content is made to the big idea of individuality and conformity.	Accurately relates ideas of individuality and conformity to assignment.	Insightfully relates the big idea of individuality and conformity to assignment.
Content	Limited or no content application.	Vague connections are made to content.	Some connections to content are made with some evidence.	Synthesizes content across lessons with substantial support and evidence.
Process	Limited or vague evidence.	Reasoning is inaccurate, lacks originality, logical conclusions, or substantial claims.	Demonstrates some evidence of higher level thinking (creativity, evaluation, or analysis).	Provides insightful evidence to support higher level thinking (creativity, evaluation, or analysis) in developing complex conclusions.
Student-Developed Criteria				

Comments:

About the Authors

Emily Mofield, Ed.D., is the lead consulting teacher for gifted education for Sumner County Schools in Tennessee and is involved in supporting several projects with Vanderbilt Programs for Talented Youth. She has also taught as a gifted education language arts middle school teacher for 10 years. Her work is devoted to developing challenging differentiated curriculum for gifted learners and addressing their social/emotional needs. Emily regularly presents professional development on effective differentiation for advanced learners. She is a national board certified teacher in Language Arts and has been recognized as the Tennessee Association for Gifted Children Teacher of the Year.

Tamra Stambaugh, Ph.D., is an assistant research professor in special education and executive director of Programs for Talented Youth at Vanderbilt University Peabody College. She received her Ph.D. in Educational Policy, Planning, and Leadership with an emphasis in gifted education from the College of William and Mary. She is the coauthor/editor of several books including *Serving Gifted Students in Rural Settings* (coedited with Susannah Wood), *Comprehensive Curriculum for Gifted Learners* (with Joyce VanTassel-Baska), *Overlooked Gems: A National Perspective on Low-Income Promising Students* (with Joyce VanTassel-Baska), *Leading Change in Gifted Education* (with Bronwyn MacFarlane), the *Jacob's Ladder Reading Comprehension Program Series* (with Joyce VanTassel-Baska and Kim Chandler), and *Practical Solutions for Underrepresented Gifted Students: Effective Curriculum* (with Kim Chandler), as well as numerous book chapters and research articles. Stambaugh's research interests focus on talent development support structures for gifted students and key curriculum and instructional interventions that support gifted learners—especially those students from rural backgrounds and those from poverty.

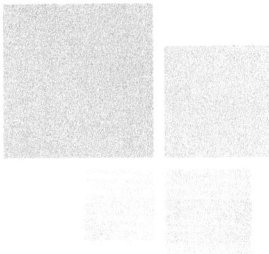

Common Core State Standards Alignment

Lesson	Common Core State Standards in ELA/Literacy
Lesson 1	RL.9-10.1 Cite strong and thorough textual evidence to support analysis of what the text says explicitly as well as inferences drawn from the text.
	RL.9-10.2 Determine a theme or central idea of a text and analyze in detail its development over the course of the text, including how it emerges and is shaped and refined by specific details; provide an objective summary of the text.
	RL.9-10.3 Analyze how complex characters (e.g., those with multiple or conflicting motivations) develop over the course of a text, interact with other characters, and advance the plot or develop the theme.
	RL.9-10.4 Determine the meaning of words and phrases as they are used in the text, including figurative and connotative meanings; analyze the cumulative impact of specific word choices on meaning and tone (e.g., how the language evokes a sense of time and place; how it sets a formal or informal tone).
	RL.9-10.5 Analyze how an author's choices concerning how to structure a text, order events within it (e.g., parallel plots), and manipulate time (e.g., pacing, flashbacks) create such effects as mystery, tension, or surprise.
	SL.9-10.1c Propel conversations by posing and responding to questions that relate the current discussion to broader themes or larger ideas; actively incorporate others into the discussion; and clarify, verify, or challenge ideas and conclusions.
	SL.9-10.1d Respond thoughtfully to diverse perspectives, summarize points of agreement and disagreement, and, when warranted, qualify or justify their own views and understanding and make new connections in light of the evidence and reasoning presented.

Lesson	Common Core State Standards in ELA/Literacy
Lesson 1, *continued*	W.9-10.4 Produce clear and coherent writing in which the development, organization, and style are appropriate to task, purpose, and audience.
Lesson 2	RL.9-10.1 Cite strong and thorough textual evidence to support analysis of what the text says explicitly as well as inferences drawn from the text.
	RL.9-10.2 Determine a theme or central idea of a text and analyze in detail its development over the course of the text, including how it emerges and is shaped and refined by specific details; provide an objective summary of the text.
	RL.9-10.3 Analyze how complex characters (e.g., those with multiple or conflicting motivations) develop over the course of a text, interact with other characters, and advance the plot or develop the theme.
	RL.9-10.4 Determine the meaning of words and phrases as they are used in the text, including figurative and connotative meanings; analyze the cumulative impact of specific word choices on meaning and tone (e.g., how the language evokes a sense of time and place; how it sets a formal or informal tone).
	RL.9-10.5 Analyze how an author's choices concerning how to structure a text, order events within it (e.g., parallel plots), and manipulate time (e.g., pacing, flashbacks) create such effects as mystery, tension, or surprise.
	SL.9-10.1 Initiate and participate effectively in a range of collaborative discussions (one-on-one, in groups, and teacher-led) with diverse partners on grades 9–10 topics, texts, and issues, building on others' ideas and expressing their own clearly and persuasively.
	SL.9-10.1c Propel conversations by posing and responding to questions that relate the current discussion to broader themes or larger ideas; actively incorporate others into the discussion; and clarify, verify, or challenge ideas and conclusions.
	SL.9-10.1d Respond thoughtfully to diverse perspectives, summarize points of agreement and disagreement, and, when warranted, qualify or justify their own views and understanding and make new connections in light of the evidence and reasoning presented.
	SL.9-10.4 Present information, findings, and supporting evidence clearly, concisely, and logically such that listeners can follow the line of reasoning and the organization, development, substance, and style are appropriate to purpose, audience, and task.
	W.9-10.4 Produce clear and coherent writing in which the development, organization, and style are appropriate to task, purpose, and audience.

Lesson	Common Core State Standards in ELA/Literacy
Lesson 3	SL.8.2 Analyze the purpose of information presented in diverse media and formats (e.g., visually, quantitatively, orally) and evaluate the motives (e.g., social, commercial, political) behind its presentation.
	SL.9-10.1 Initiate and participate effectively in a range of collaborative discussions (one-on-one, in groups, and teacher-led) with diverse partners on grades 9–10 topics, texts, and issues, building on others' ideas and expressing their own clearly and persuasively.
	SL.9-10.1c Propel conversations by posing and responding to questions that relate the current discussion to broader themes or larger ideas; actively incorporate others into the discussion; and clarify, verify, or challenge ideas and conclusions.
	SL.9-10.1d Respond thoughtfully to diverse perspectives, summarize points of agreement and disagreement, and, when warranted, qualify or justify their own views and understanding and make new connections in light of the evidence and reasoning presented.
	W.9-10.4 Produce clear and coherent writing in which the development, organization, and style are appropriate to task, purpose, and audience.
	RI.9-10.7 Analyze various accounts of a subject told in different mediums (e.g., a person's life story in both print and multimedia), determining which details are emphasized in each account.
Lesson 4	RI.9-10.1 Cite strong and thorough textual evidence to support analysis of what the text says explicitly as well as inferences drawn from the text.
	RI.9-10.2 Determine a central idea of a text and analyze its development over the course of the text, including how it emerges and is shaped and refined by specific details; provide an objective summary of the text.
	RI.9-10.3 Analyze how the author unfolds an analysis or series of ideas or events, including the order in which the points are made, how they are introduced and developed, and the connections that are drawn between them.
	RI.9-10.6 Determine an author's point of view or purpose in a text and analyze how an author uses rhetoric to advance that point of view or purpose.
	RI.9-10.7 Analyze various accounts of a subject told in different mediums (e.g., a person's life story in both print and multimedia), determining which details are emphasized in each account.

Lesson	Common Core State Standards in ELA/Literacy
Lesson 4, *continued*	RI.9-10.9 Analyze seminal U.S. documents of historical and literary significance (e.g., Washington's Farewell Address, the Gettysburg Address, Roosevelt's Four Freedoms speech, King's "Letter from Birmingham Jail"), including how they address related themes and concepts.
	SL.9-10.1 Initiate and participate effectively in a range of collaborative discussions (one-on-one, in groups, and teacher-led) with diverse partners on grades 9–10 topics, texts, and issues, building on others' ideas and expressing their own clearly and persuasively.
	SL.9-10.1c Propel conversations by posing and responding to questions that relate the current discussion to broader themes or larger ideas; actively incorporate others into the discussion; and clarify, verify, or challenge ideas and conclusions.
	SL.9-10.1d Respond thoughtfully to diverse perspectives, summarize points of agreement and disagreement, and, when warranted, qualify or justify their own views and understanding and make new connections in light of the evidence and reasoning presented.
	RH.9-10.1 Cite specific textual evidence to support analysis of primary and secondary sources, attending to such features as the date and origin of the information.
	RH.9-10.2 Determine the central ideas or information of a primary or secondary source; provide an accurate summary of how key events or ideas develop over the course of the text.
	RH.9-10.8 Assess the extent to which the reasoning and evidence in a text support the author's claims.
	RH.9-10.9 Compare and contrast treatments of the same topic in several primary and secondary sources.
	W.9-10.4 Produce clear and coherent writing in which the development, organization, and style are appropriate to task, purpose, and audience.
Lesson 5	RI.9-10.1 Cite strong and thorough textual evidence to support analysis of what the text says explicitly as well as inferences drawn from the text.
	RI.9-10.3 Analyze how the author unfolds an analysis or series of ideas or events, including the order in which the points are made, how they are introduced and developed, and the connections that are drawn between them.
	RI.9-10.7 Analyze various accounts of a subject told in different mediums (e.g., a person's life story in both print and multimedia), determining which details are emphasized in each account.

Lesson	Common Core State Standards in ELA/Literacy
Lesson 5, *continued*	SL.8.2 Analyze the purpose of information presented in diverse media and formats (e.g., visually, quantitatively, orally) and evaluate the motives (e.g., social, commercial, political) behind its presentation.
	SL.9-10.1 Initiate and participate effectively in a range of collaborative discussions (one-on-one, in groups, and teacher-led) with diverse partners on grades 9–10 topics, texts, and issues, building on others' ideas and expressing their own clearly and persuasively.
	SL.9-10.1c Propel conversations by posing and responding to questions that relate the current discussion to broader themes or larger ideas; actively incorporate others into the discussion; and clarify, verify, or challenge ideas and conclusions.
	SL.9-10.1d Respond thoughtfully to diverse perspectives, summarize points of agreement and disagreement, and, when warranted, qualify or justify their own views and understanding and make new connections in light of the evidence and reasoning presented.
	W.9-10.4 Produce clear and coherent writing in which the development, organization, and style are appropriate to task, purpose, and audience.
Lesson 6	RL.9-10.1 Cite strong and thorough textual evidence to support analysis of what the text says explicitly as well as inferences drawn from the text.
	RL.9-10.2 Determine a theme or central idea of a text and analyze in detail its development over the course of the text, including how it emerges and is shaped and refined by specific details; provide an objective summary of the text.
	RL.9-10.4 Determine the meaning of words and phrases as they are used in the text, including figurative and connotative meanings; analyze the cumulative impact of specific word choices on meaning and tone (e.g., how the language evokes a sense of time and place; how it sets a formal or informal tone).
	SL.9-10.1 Initiate and participate effectively in a range of collaborative discussions (one-on-one, in groups, and teacher-led) with diverse partners on grades 9–10 topics, texts, and issues, building on others' ideas and expressing their own clearly and persuasively.
	SL.9-10.1c Propel conversations by posing and responding to questions that relate the current discussion to broader themes or larger ideas; actively incorporate others into the discussion; and clarify, verify, or challenge ideas and conclusions.

Lesson	Common Core State Standards in ELA/Literacy
Lesson 6, *continued*	SL.9-10.1d Respond thoughtfully to diverse perspectives, summarize points of agreement and disagreement, and, when warranted, qualify or justify their own views and understanding and make new connections in light of the evidence and reasoning presented.
	SL.9-10.4 Present information, findings, and supporting evidence clearly, concisely, and logically such that listeners can follow the line of reasoning and the organization, development, substance, and style are appropriate to purpose, audience, and task.
	W.9-10.4 Produce clear and coherent writing in which the development, organization, and style are appropriate to task, purpose, and audience.
Lesson 7	RI.9-10.1 Cite strong and thorough textual evidence to support analysis of what the text says explicitly as well as inferences drawn from the text.
	RI.9-10.2 Determine a central idea of a text and analyze its development over the course of the text, including how it emerges and is shaped and refined by specific details; provide an objective summary of the text.
	RI.9-10.3 Analyze how the author unfolds an analysis or series of ideas or events, including the order in which the points are made, how they are introduced and developed, and the connections that are drawn between them.
	RI.9-10.5 Analyze in detail how an author's ideas or claims are developed and refined by particular sentences, paragraphs, or larger portions of a text (e.g., a section or chapter).
	RI.9-10.6 Determine an author's point of view or purpose in a text and analyze how an author uses rhetoric to advance that point of view or purpose.
	RI.9-10.9 Analyze seminal U.S. documents of historical and literary significance (e.g., Washington's Farewell Address, the Gettysburg Address, Roosevelt's Four Freedoms speech, King's "Letter from Birmingham Jail"), including how they address related themes and concepts.
	SL.9-10.1 Initiate and participate effectively in a range of collaborative discussions (one-on-one, in groups, and teacher-led) with diverse partners on grades 9–10 topics, texts, and issues, building on others' ideas and expressing their own clearly and persuasively.
	SL.9-10.1c Propel conversations by posing and responding to questions that relate the current discussion to broader themes or larger ideas; actively incorporate others into the discussion; and clarify, verify, or challenge ideas and conclusions.

Lesson	Common Core State Standards in ELA/Literacy
Lesson 7, *continued*	SL.9-10.1d Respond thoughtfully to diverse perspectives, summarize points of agreement and disagreement, and, when warranted, qualify or justify their own views and understanding and make new connections in light of the evidence and reasoning presented.
	RH.9-10.1 Cite specific textual evidence to support analysis of primary and secondary sources, attending to such features as the date and origin of the information.
	RH.9-10.2 Determine the central ideas or information of a primary or secondary source; provide an accurate summary of how key events or ideas develop over the course of the text.
	RH.9-10.5 Analyze how a text uses structure to emphasize key points or advance an explanation or analysis.
	RH.9-10.8 Assess the extent to which the reasoning and evidence in a text support the author's claims.
	RH.9-10.9 Compare and contrast treatments of the same topic in several primary and secondary sources.
	W.9-10.4 Produce clear and coherent writing in which the development, organization, and style are appropriate to task, purpose, and audience.
Lesson 8	RL.9-10.1 Cite strong and thorough textual evidence to support analysis of what the text says explicitly as well as inferences drawn from the text.
	RL.9-10.2 Determine a theme or central idea of a text and analyze in detail its development over the course of the text, including how it emerges and is shaped and refined by specific details; provide an objective summary of the text.
	RL.9-10.4 Determine the meaning of words and phrases as they are used in the text, including figurative and connotative meanings; analyze the cumulative impact of specific word choices on meaning and tone (e.g., how the language evokes a sense of time and place; how it sets a formal or informal tone).
	SL.9-10.1 Initiate and participate effectively in a range of collaborative discussions (one-on-one, in groups, and teacher-led) with diverse partners on grades 9–10 topics, texts, and issues, building on others' ideas and expressing their own clearly and persuasively.
	SL.9-10.1c Propel conversations by posing and responding to questions that relate the current discussion to broader themes or larger ideas; actively incorporate others into the discussion; and clarify, verify, or challenge ideas and conclusions.

212

Lesson	Common Core State Standards in ELA/Literacy
Lesson 8, *continued*	SL.9-10.1d Respond thoughtfully to diverse perspectives, summarize points of agreement and disagreement, and, when warranted, qualify or justify their own views and understanding and make new connections in light of the evidence and reasoning presented.
	SL.9-10.4 Present information, findings, and supporting evidence clearly, concisely, and logically such that listeners can follow the line of reasoning and the organization, development, substance, and style are appropriate to purpose, audience, and task.
	W.9-10.4 Produce clear and coherent writing in which the development, organization, and style are appropriate to task, purpose, and audience.
Lesson 9	RL.9-10.1 Cite strong and thorough textual evidence to support analysis of what the text says explicitly as well as inferences drawn from the text.
	RL.9-10.2 Determine a theme or central idea of a text and analyze in detail its development over the course of the text, including how it emerges and is shaped and refined by specific details; provide an objective summary of the text.
	RL.9-10.3 Analyze how complex characters (e.g., those with multiple or conflicting motivations) develop over the course of a text, interact with other characters, and advance the plot or develop the theme.
	RL.9-10.4 Determine the meaning of words and phrases as they are used in the text, including figurative and connotative meanings; analyze the cumulative impact of specific word choices on meaning and tone (e.g., how the language evokes a sense of time and place; how it sets a formal or informal tone).
	SL.9-10.1 Initiate and participate effectively in a range of collaborative discussions (one-on-one, in groups, and teacher-led) with diverse partners on grades 9–10 topics, texts, and issues, building on others' ideas and expressing their own clearly and persuasively.
	SL.9-10.1c Propel conversations by posing and responding to questions that relate the current discussion to broader themes or larger ideas; actively incorporate others into the discussion; and clarify, verify, or challenge ideas and conclusions.
	SL.9-10.1d Respond thoughtfully to diverse perspectives, summarize points of agreement and disagreement, and, when warranted, qualify or justify their own views and understanding and make new connections in light of the evidence and reasoning presented.

Lesson	Common Core State Standards in ELA/Literacy	213
Lesson 9, *continued*	SL.9-10.4 Present information, findings, and supporting evidence clearly, concisely, and logically such that listeners can follow the line of reasoning and the organization, development, substance, and style are appropriate to purpose, audience, and task.	
	W.9-10.4 Produce clear and coherent writing in which the development, organization, and style are appropriate to task, purpose, and audience.	
Lesson 10	RI.9-10.1 Cite strong and thorough textual evidence to support analysis of what the text says explicitly as well as inferences drawn from the text.	
	RI.9-10.2 Determine a central idea of a text and analyze its development over the course of the text, including how it emerges and is shaped and refined by specific details; provide an objective summary of the text.	
	RI.9-10.3 Analyze how the author unfolds an analysis or series of ideas or events, including the order in which the points are made, how they are introduced and developed, and the connections that are drawn between them.	
	RI.9-10.4 Determine the meaning of words and phrases as they are used in a text, including figurative, connotative, and technical meanings; analyze the cumulative impact of specific word choices on meaning and tone (e.g., how the language of a court opinion differs from that of a newspaper).	
	RI.9-10.5 Analyze in detail how an author's ideas or claims are developed and refined by particular sentences, paragraphs, or larger portions of a text (e.g., a section or chapter).	
	RI.9-10.6 Determine an author's point of view or purpose in a text and analyze how an author uses rhetoric to advance that point of view or purpose.	
	RI.9-10.9 Analyze seminal U.S. documents of historical and literary significance (e.g., Washington's Farewell Address, the Gettysburg Address, Roosevelt's Four Freedoms speech, King's "Letter from Birmingham Jail"), including how they address related themes and concepts.	
	SL.9-10.1 Initiate and participate effectively in a range of collaborative discussions (one-on-one, in groups, and teacher-led) with diverse partners on grades 9–10 topics, texts, and issues, building on others' ideas and expressing their own clearly and persuasively.	
	SL.9-10.1c Propel conversations by posing and responding to questions that relate the current discussion to broader themes or larger ideas; actively incorporate others into the discussion; and clarify, verify, or challenge ideas and conclusions.	

Lesson	Common Core State Standards in ELA/Literacy
Lesson 10, *continued*	SL.9-10.1d Respond thoughtfully to diverse perspectives, summarize points of agreement and disagreement, and, when warranted, qualify or justify their own views and understanding and make new connections in light of the evidence and reasoning presented.
	RH.9-10.1 Cite specific textual evidence to support analysis of primary and secondary sources, attending to such features as the date and origin of the information.
	RH.9-10.2 Determine the central ideas or information of a primary or secondary source; provide an accurate summary of how key events or ideas develop over the course of the text.
	RH.9-10.4 Determine the meaning of words and phrases as they are used in a text, including vocabulary describing political, social, or economic aspects of history/social science.
	RH.9-10.5 Analyze how a text uses structure to emphasize key points or advance an explanation or analysis.
	RH.9-10.8 Assess the extent to which the reasoning and evidence in a text support the author's claims.
	RH.9-10.9 Compare and contrast treatments of the same topic in several primary and secondary sources.
	W.9-10.4 Produce clear and coherent writing in which the development, organization, and style are appropriate to task, purpose, and audience.
Lesson 11	RI.9-10.1 Cite strong and thorough textual evidence to support analysis of what the text says explicitly as well as inferences drawn from the text.
	RI.9-10.2 Determine a central idea of a text and analyze its development over the course of the text, including how it emerges and is shaped and refined by specific details; provide an objective summary of the text.
	RI.9-10.3 Analyze how the author unfolds an analysis or series of ideas or events, including the order in which the points are made, how they are introduced and developed, and the connections that are drawn between them.
	RI.9-10.4 Determine the meaning of words and phrases as they are used in a text, including figurative, connotative, and technical meanings; analyze the cumulative impact of specific word choices on meaning and tone (e.g., how the language of a court opinion differs from that of a newspaper).
	RI.9-10.5 Analyze in detail how an author's ideas or claims are developed and refined by particular sentences, paragraphs, or larger portions of a text (e.g., a section or chapter). RI.9-10.6 Determine an author's point of view or purpose in a text and analyze how an author uses rhetoric to advance that point of view or purpose.

Lesson	Common Core State Standards in ELA/Literacy
Lesson 11, *continued*	RI.9-10.7 Analyze various accounts of a subject told in different mediums (e.g., a person's life story in both print and multimedia), determining which details are emphasized in each account.
	RI.9-10.9 Analyze seminal U.S. documents of historical and literary significance (e.g., Washington's Farewell Address, the Gettysburg Address, Roosevelt's Four Freedoms speech, King's "Letter from Birmingham Jail"), including how they address related themes and concepts.
	SL.9-10.1 Initiate and participate effectively in a range of collaborative discussions (one-on-one, in groups, and teacher-led) with diverse partners on grades 9–10 topics, texts, and issues, building on others' ideas and expressing their own clearly and persuasively.
	SL.9-10.1c Propel conversations by posing and responding to questions that relate the current discussion to broader themes or larger ideas; actively incorporate others into the discussion; and clarify, verify, or challenge ideas and conclusions.
	SL.9-10.1d Respond thoughtfully to diverse perspectives, summarize points of agreement and disagreement, and, when warranted, qualify or justify their own views and understanding and make new connections in light of the evidence and reasoning presented.
	RH.9-10.1 Cite specific textual evidence to support analysis of primary and secondary sources, attending to such features as the date and origin of the information.
	RH.9-10.2 Determine the central ideas or information of a primary or secondary source; provide an accurate summary of how key events or ideas develop over the course of the text.
	RH.9-10.4 Determine the meaning of words and phrases as they are used in a text, including vocabulary describing political, social, or economic aspects of history/social science.
	RH.9-10.5 Analyze how a text uses structure to emphasize key points or advance an explanation or analysis.
	RH.9-10.8 Assess the extent to which the reasoning and evidence in a text support the author's claims.
	RH.9-10.9 Compare and contrast treatments of the same topic in several primary and secondary sources.
	W.9-10.4 Produce clear and coherent writing in which the development, organization, and style are appropriate to task, purpose, and audience.
Lesson 12	Varies based on product choice.

For Product Safety Concerns and Information please contact our EU
representative GPSR@taylorandfrancis.com
Taylor & Francis Verlag GmbH, Kaufingerstraße 24, 80331 München, Germany

www.ingramcontent.com/pod-product-compliance
Lightning Source LLC
Chambersburg PA
CBHW080236270326
41926CB00020B/4266